Turtles Original Prints

Mother Earth Series

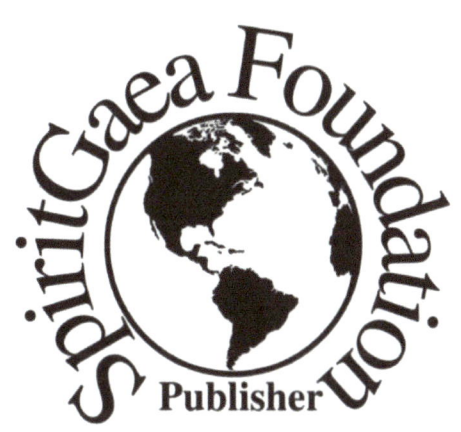 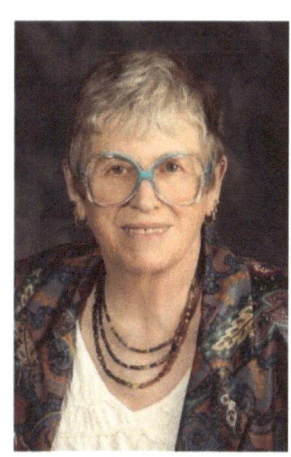

Author Artist   Jeri Lee C.Ht.

Copyright JeriLee.Com
2023
All Rights Reserved
ISBN: 9798388421203

Watercolor Art Originals

Watercolor painting is an expressive and unique form of Art that has been used to create beautiful works throughout history. It involves using thin, transparent water-based paints to create vivid images on paper or canvas surfaces. Watercolor paintings often feature soft color blends and delicate brushstrokes that lend a dreamy, romantic quality to the artwork. The vibrant colors used in this type of painting can evoke strong emotions from viewers, making it a popular choice for many artists seeking to express their innermost feelings through visual means.

Watercolor Art is a beautiful medium to capture the magic and life of nature. Using watercolors, artists can create soft, delicate washes that mimic the subtle colors of plants and animals. Watercolors blend easily with other media, such as ink or pencils, to add texture and detail. With practice, an artist can use watercolor paints to portray flowers, trees, mountains, rivers, and more with realistic depth and color.

This form of Art can bring a unique and beautiful element to any wall in your home. Whether you are looking for a tranquil landscape, vibrant flowers, or abstract shapes, there is sure to be something that captures the spirit of nature and brings joy to your space. This versatile medium will provide an eye-catching addition to any room in your home.

At age 84, I am attempting to replicate Grandma Moses with my unique version of watercolor originals. Please follow my Mother Nature Series. And if they please you, please post me a positive review.
Thank you JeriLee.Com

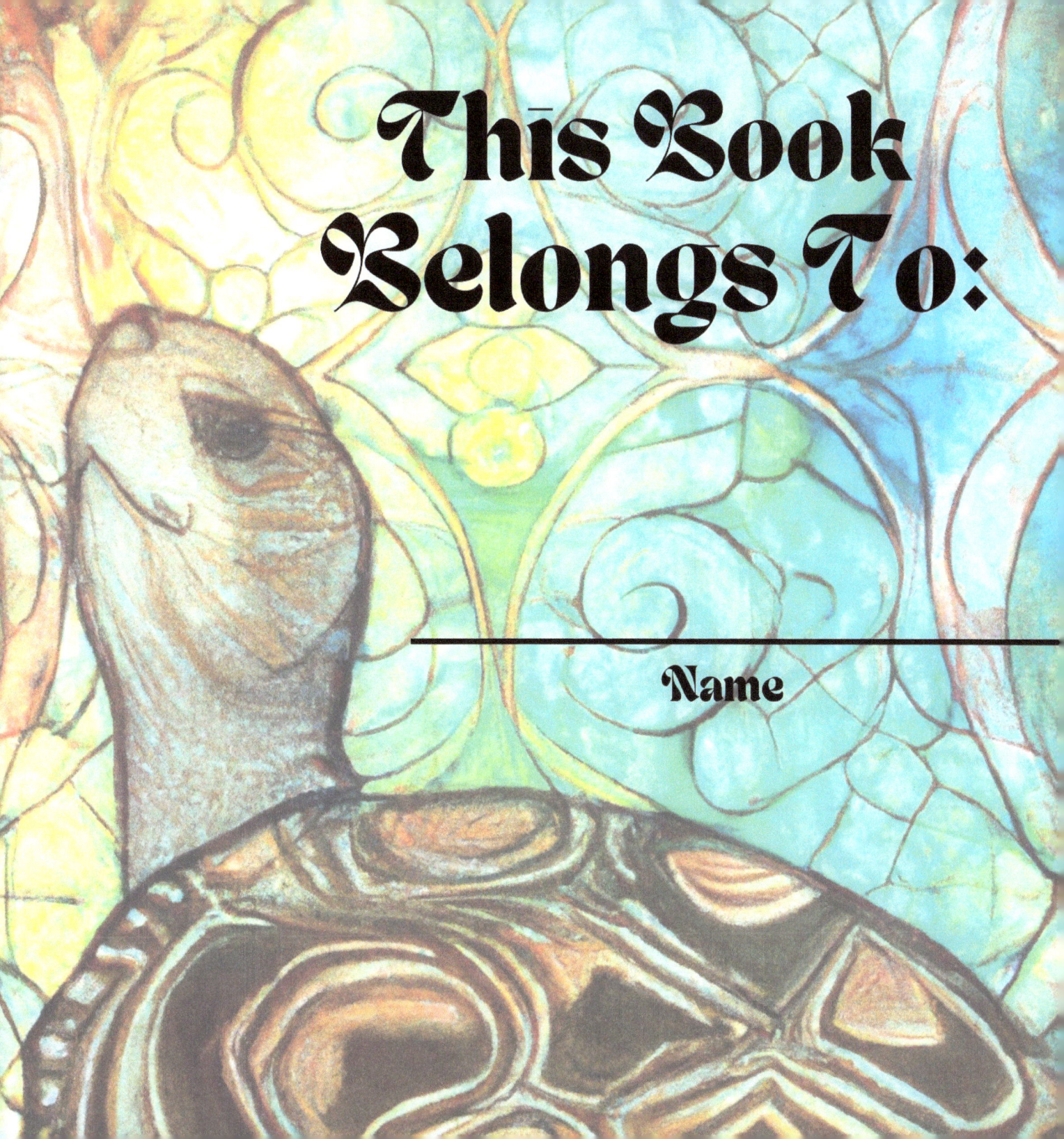

Turtles

The world is home to some of the most incredible creatures, including turtles. Unfortunately, many species of turtles are threatened or endangered due to human activities such as habitat destruction and poaching. As a result, conservation efforts have become increasingly important to protect these ancient and beloved animals. One of the most threatened turtle species is the leatherback sea turtle (Dermochelys coriacea). This sizeable marine reptile can be found in temperate and tropical waters worldwide, but it is particularly vulnerable because it has few safe nesting areas left due to coastal development. Other threats include entanglement in fishing nets, pollution from oil spills, climate change, and illegal harvesting of its meat and eggs. The hawksbill sea turtle (Eretmochelys imbricata) is another critically endangered species that face multiple threats, including habitat loss due to coastal development and tourism, over-harvesting for their shells which are used for decorative items such as jewelry or combs, accidental capture by fisheries targeting other species, egg collection by humans and predation by non-native predators such as rats or cats released into their habitats by people. The loggerhead sea turtle (Caretta caretta) also faces numerous threats, including ocean debris that they may ingest while feeding on jellyfish; boat strikes; accidental capture in shrimp trawl nets; egg collection; beachfront lighting that disorients hatchlings leading them away from the ocean instead towards roads where they may be killed; diseases spread through contact with humans who interact with them at nesting sites or during release events after being accidentally caught in fishing gear; global warming which affects both water temperature and food availability. In addition to these three main types of sea turtles, several other varieties face similar dangers, such as flatbacks & green turtles. The good news is that all countries have agreed upon regulations designed to protect these animals under international law, although enforcement varies widely depending on location & resources available for implementation. Conservation organizations like Sea Turtle Conservancy continue working hard towards preserving remaining populations & helping them thrive once again!

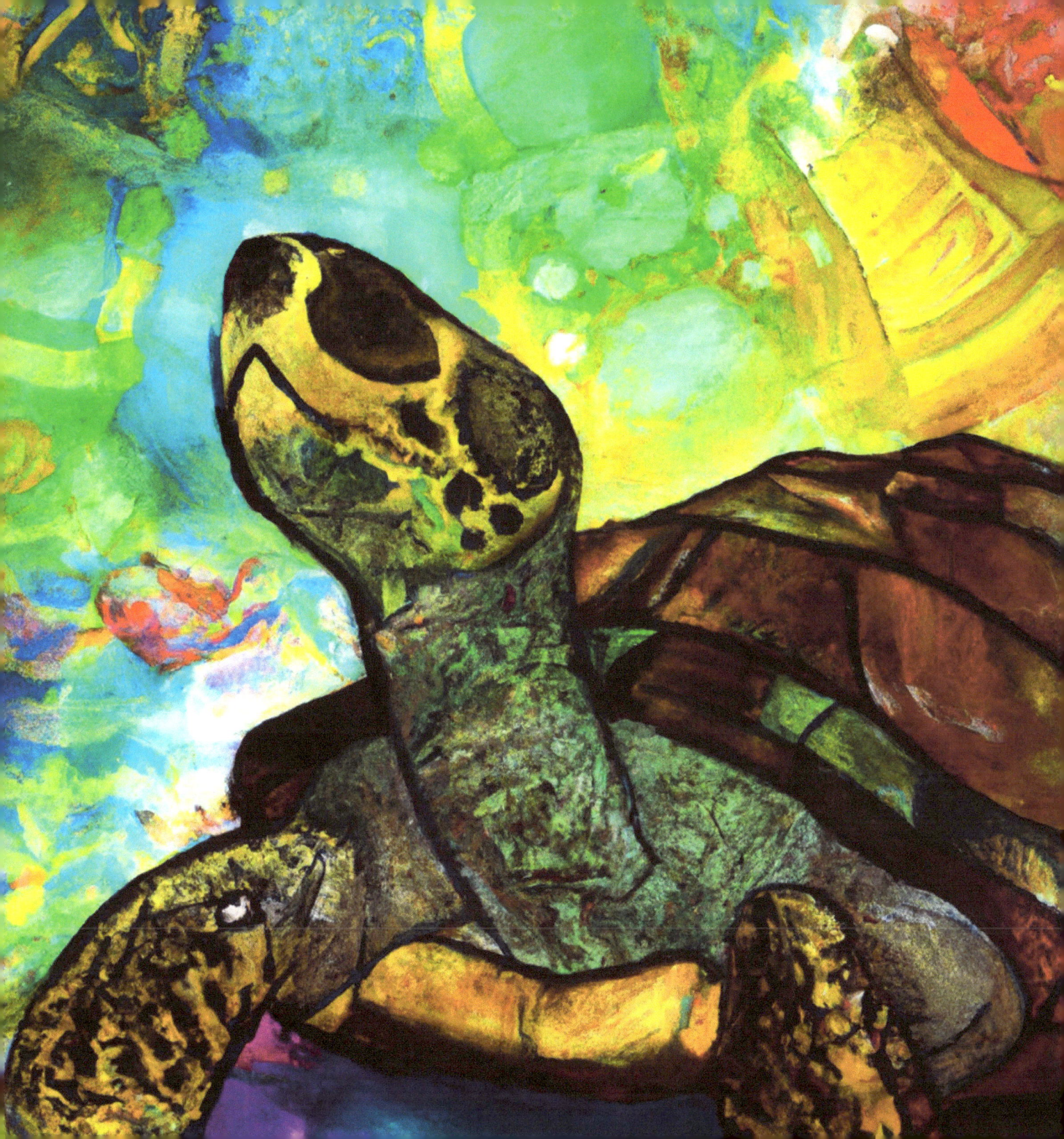

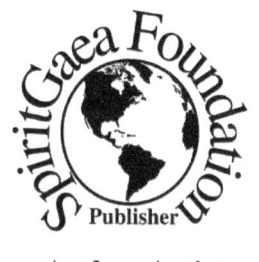

Author Artist

**Original Art
by Jeri Lee**

Copyright Jerilee.com
2022
All rights Reserved

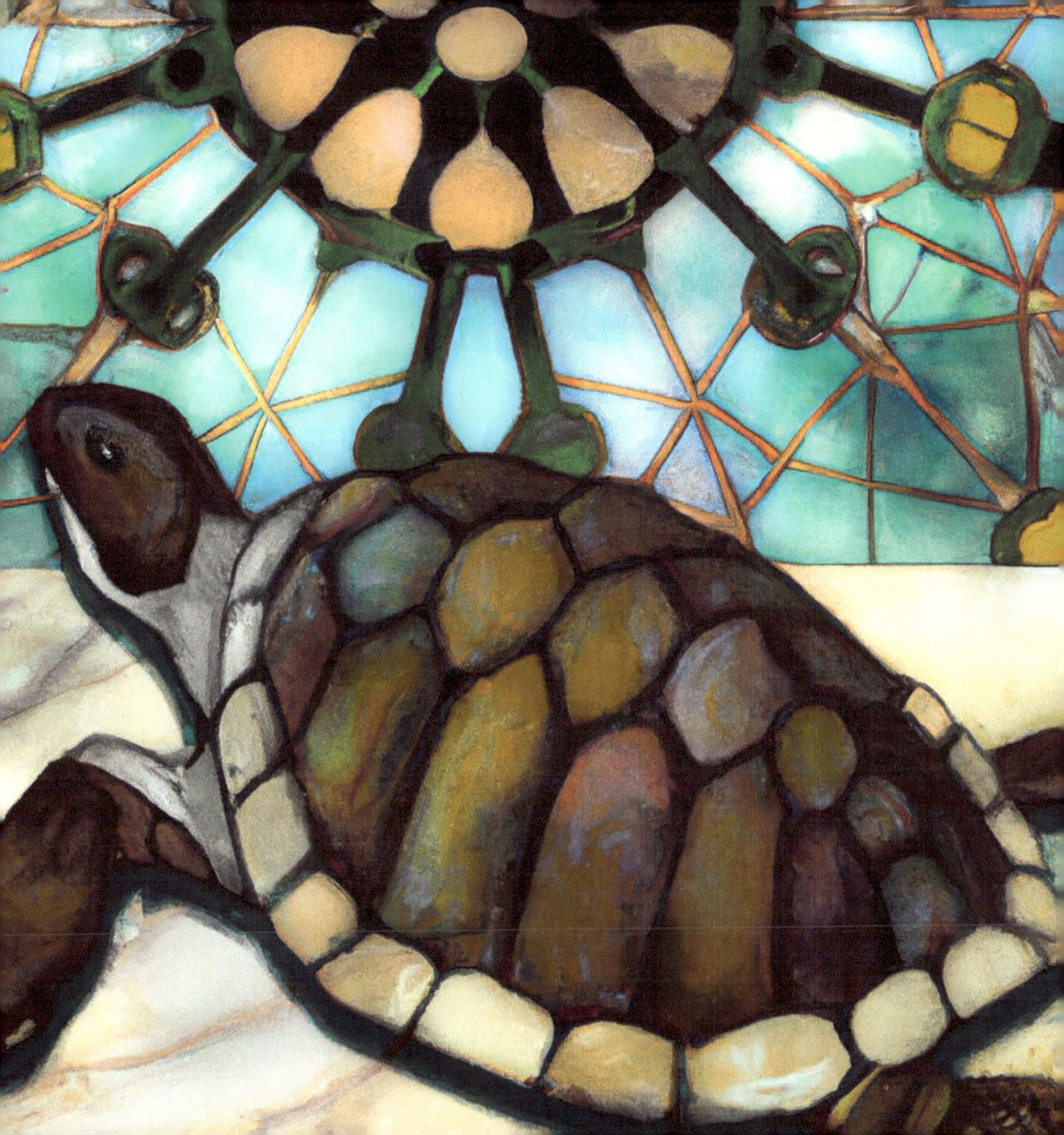

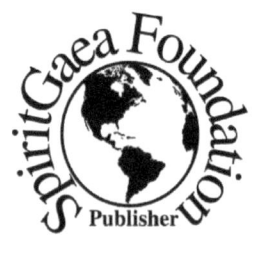

Author Artist

**Original Art
by Jeri Lee**

Copyright Jerilee.com
2022
All rights Reserved

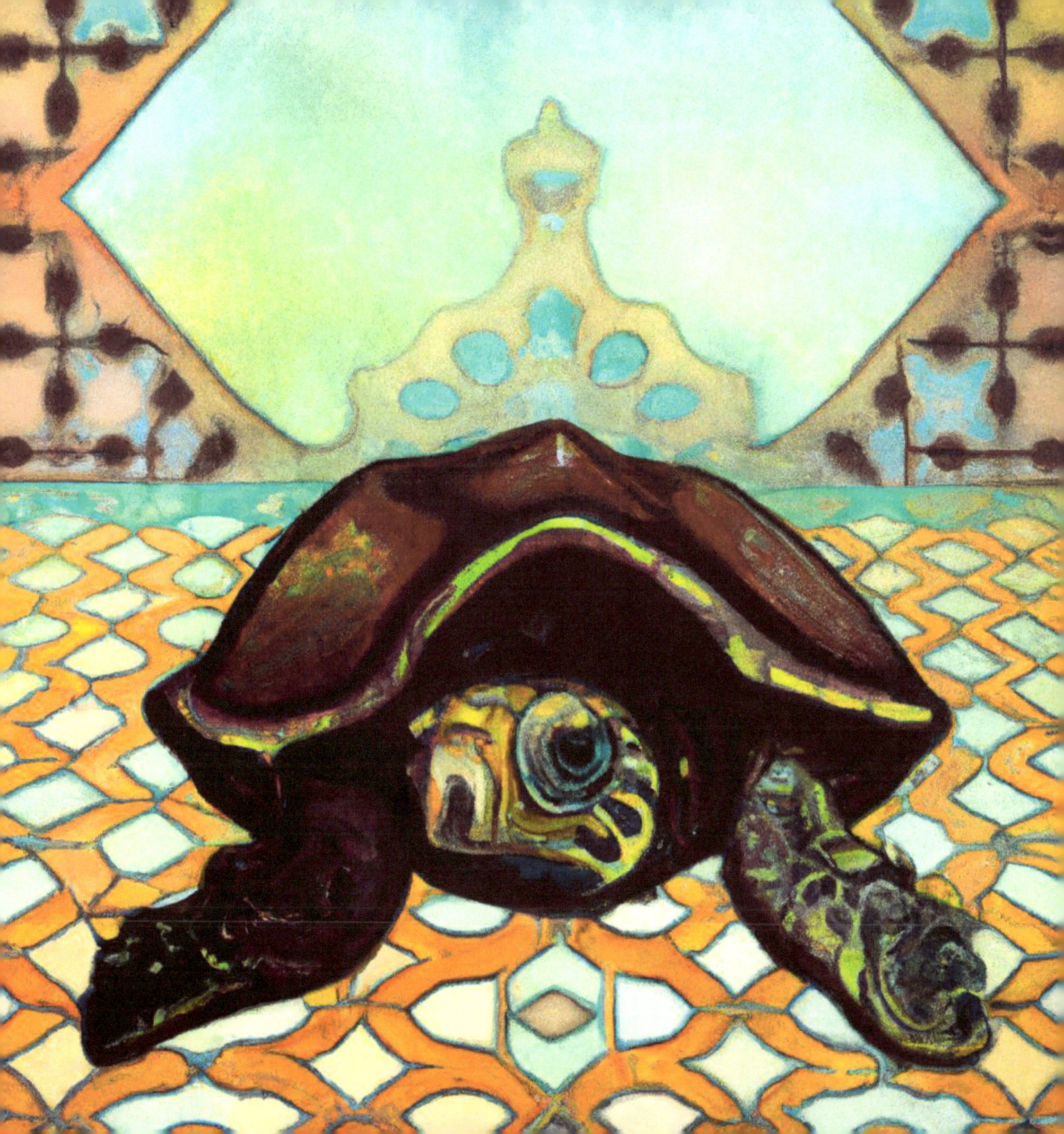

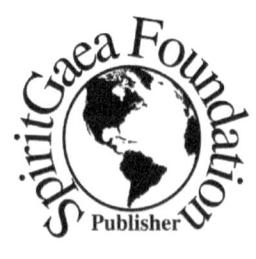

Author Artist

**Original Art
by Jeri Lee**

Copyright Jerilee.com
2022
All rights Reserved

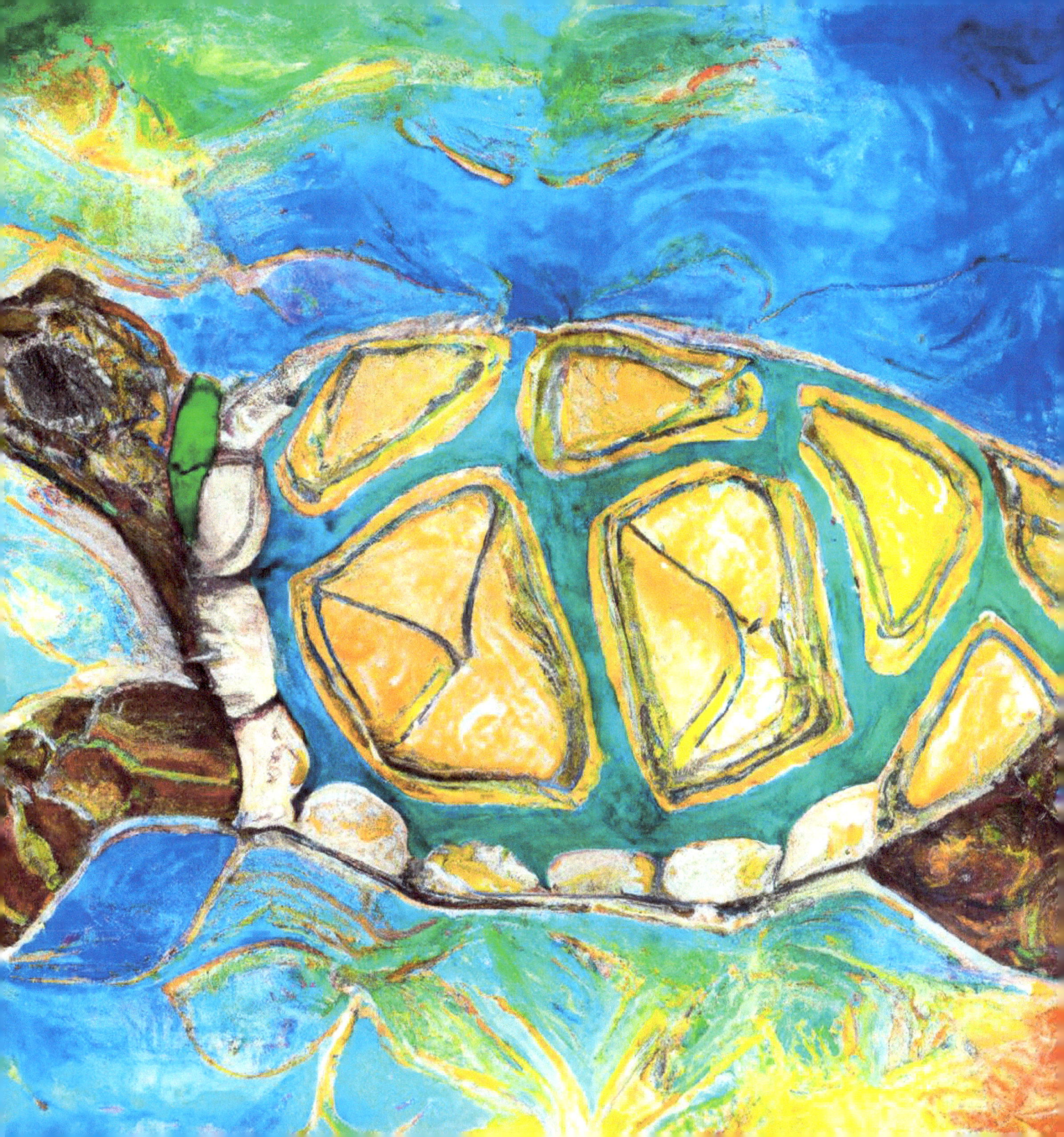

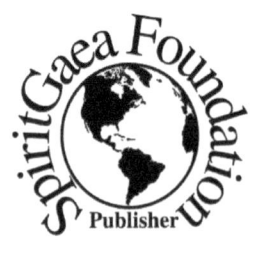

**Original Art
by Jeri Lee**

Copyright Jerilee.com
2022
All rights Reserved

Author Artist

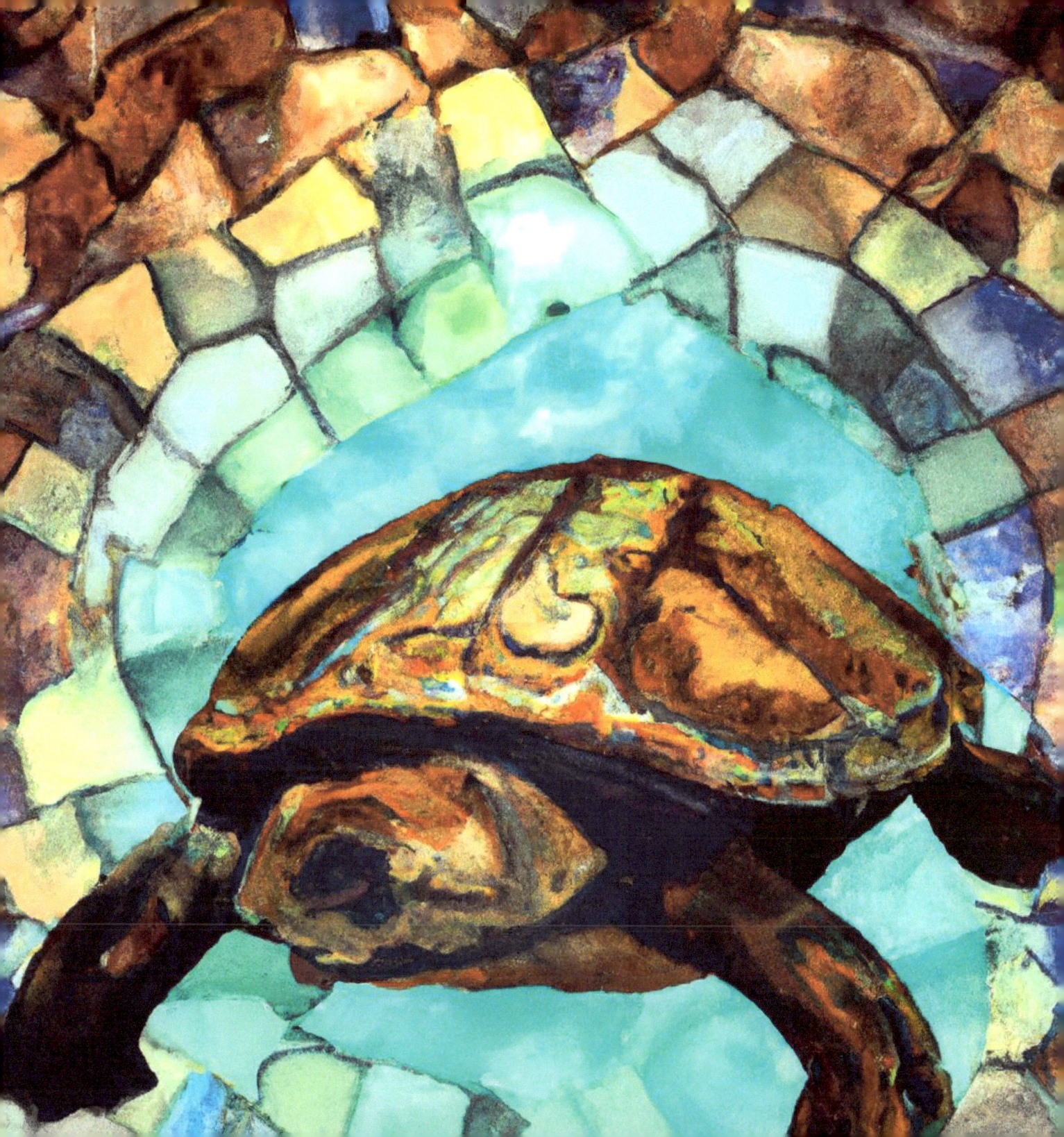

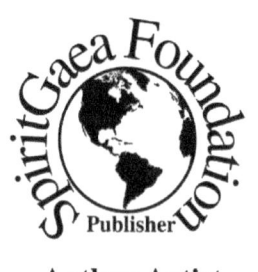

Author Artist

**Original Art
by Jeri Lee**

Copyright Jerilee.com
2022
All rights Reserved

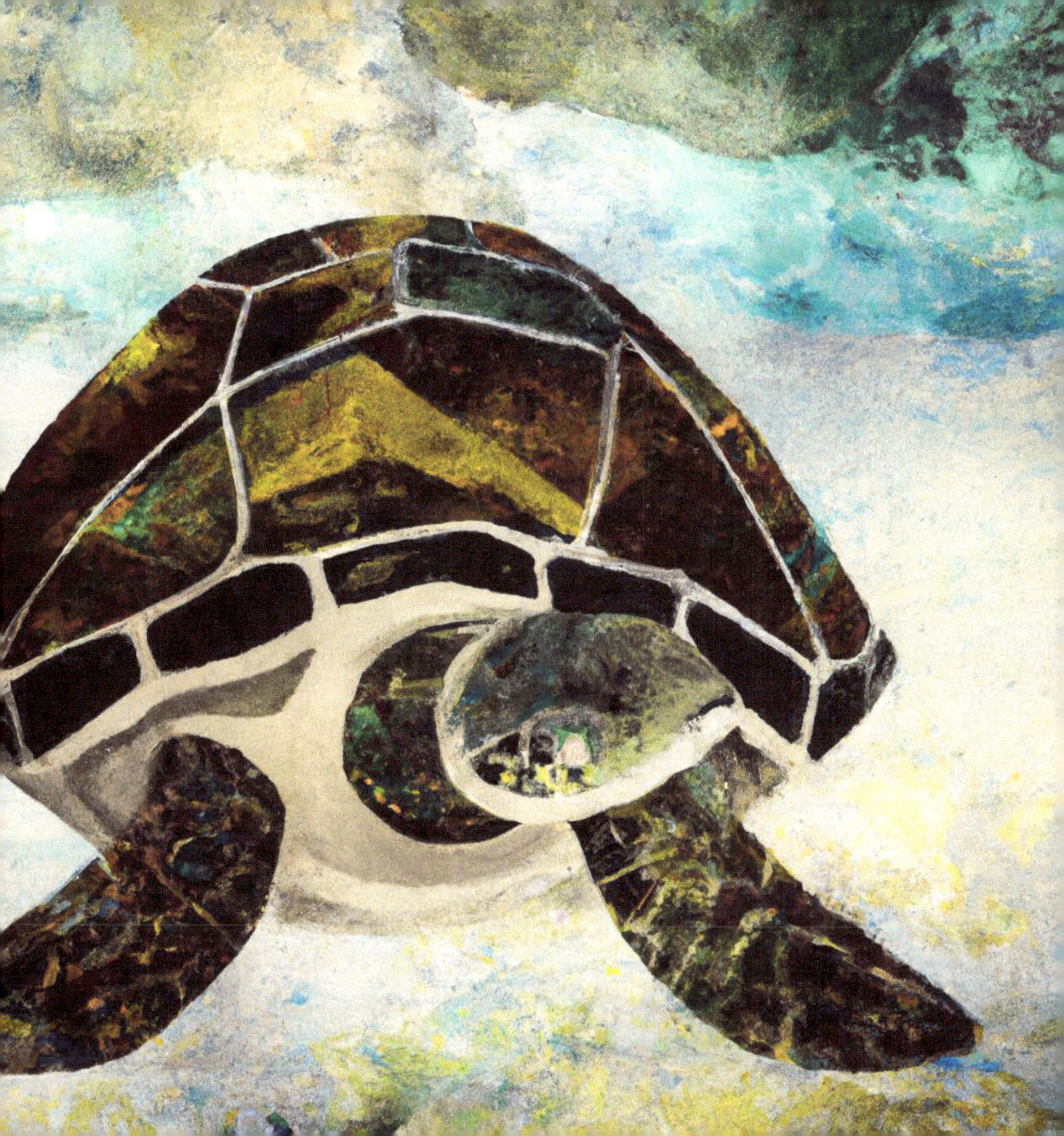

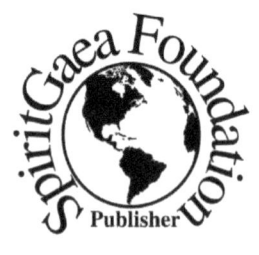

Author Artist

**Original Art
by Jeri Lee**

Copyright Jerilee.com
2022
All rights Reserved

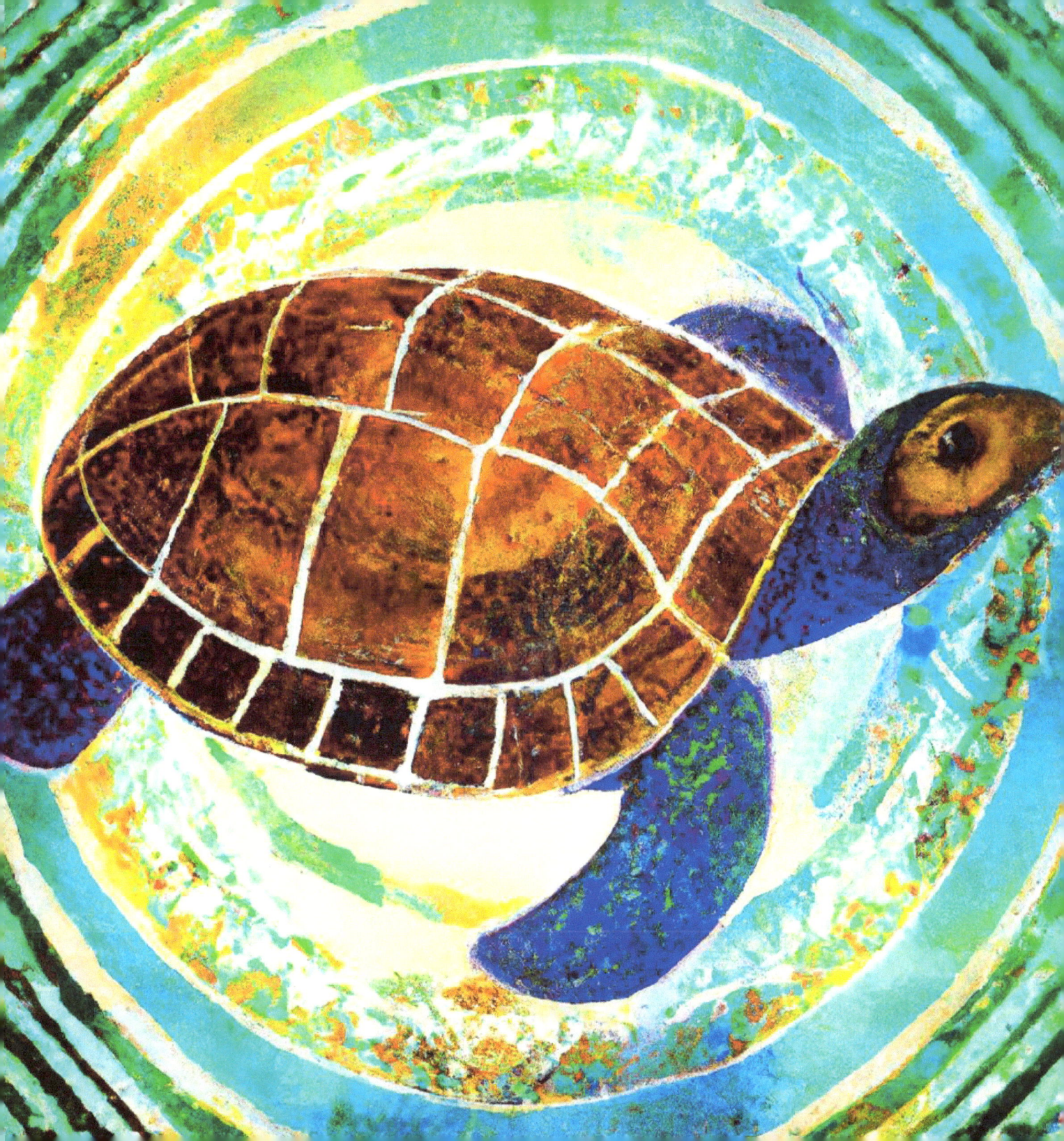

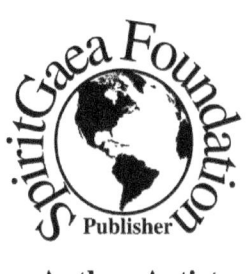

Author Artist

**Original Art
by Jeri Lee**

Copyright Jerilee.com
2022
All rights Reserved

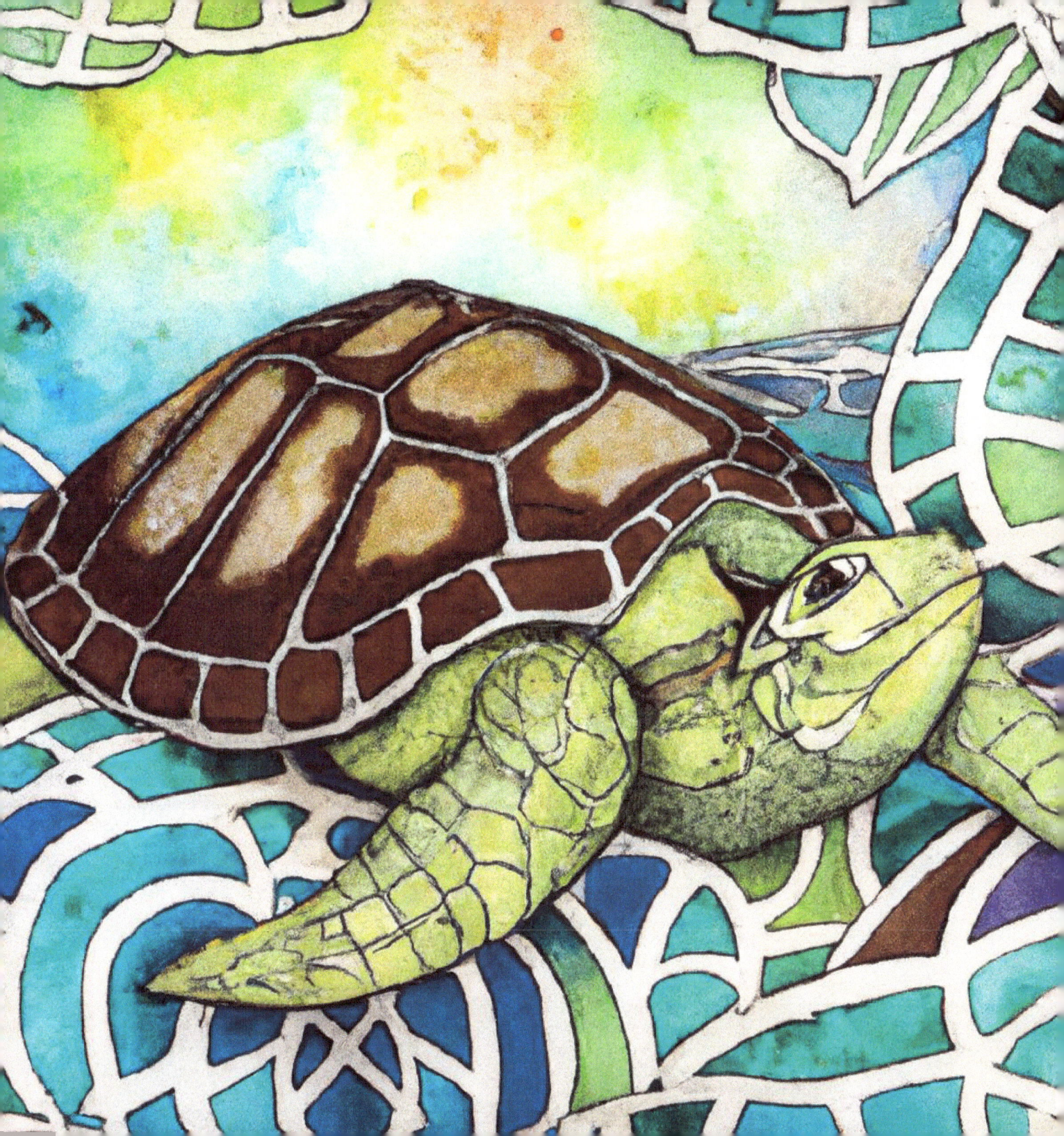

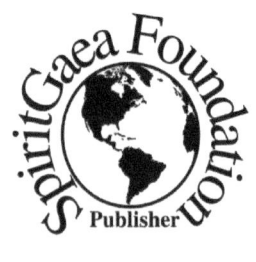

Author Artist

**Original Art
by Jeri Lee**

Copyright Jerilee.com
2022
All rights Reserved

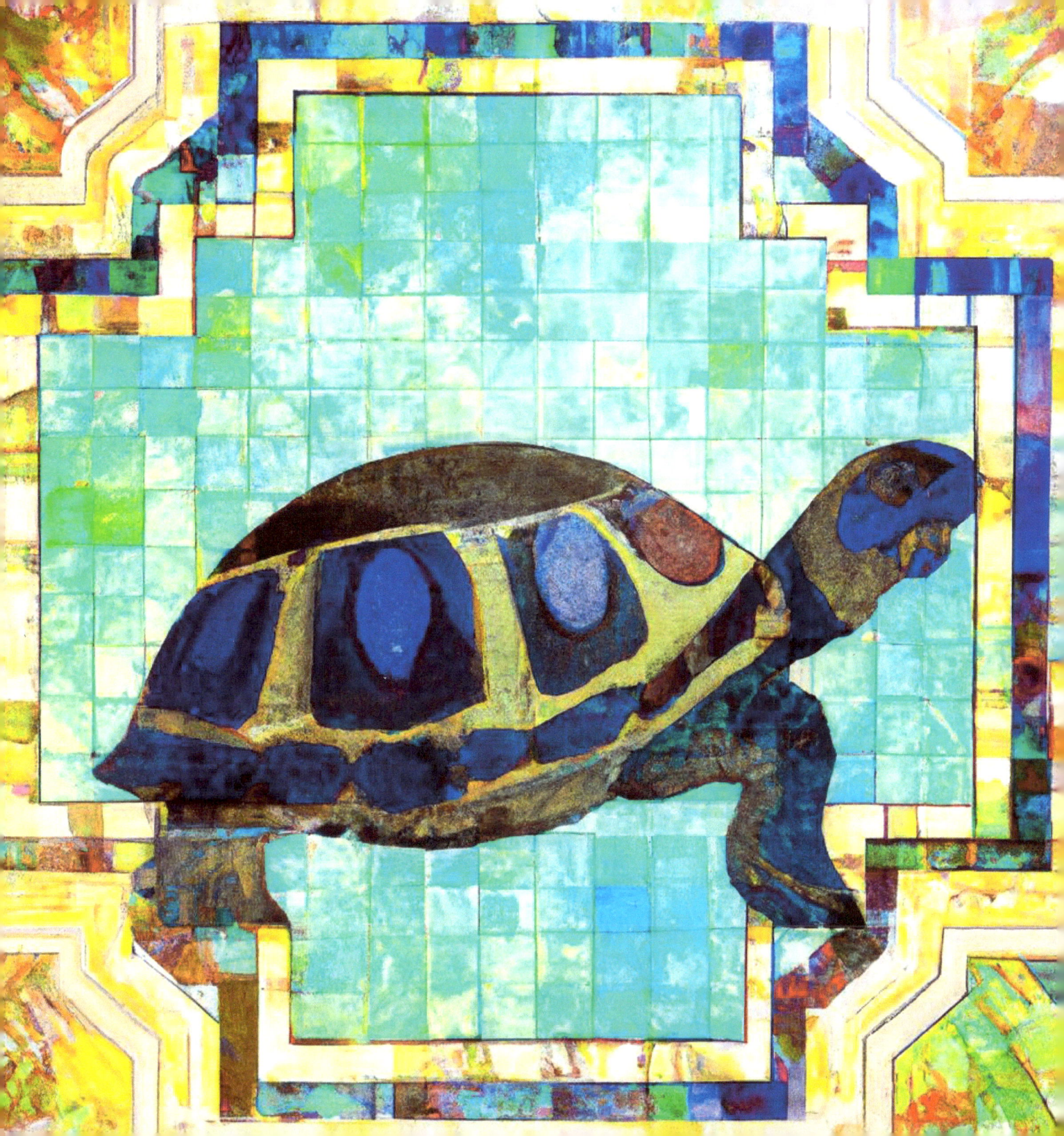

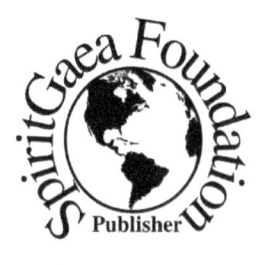

Author Artist

**Original Art
by Jeri Lee**

Copyright Jerilee.com
2022
All rights Reserved

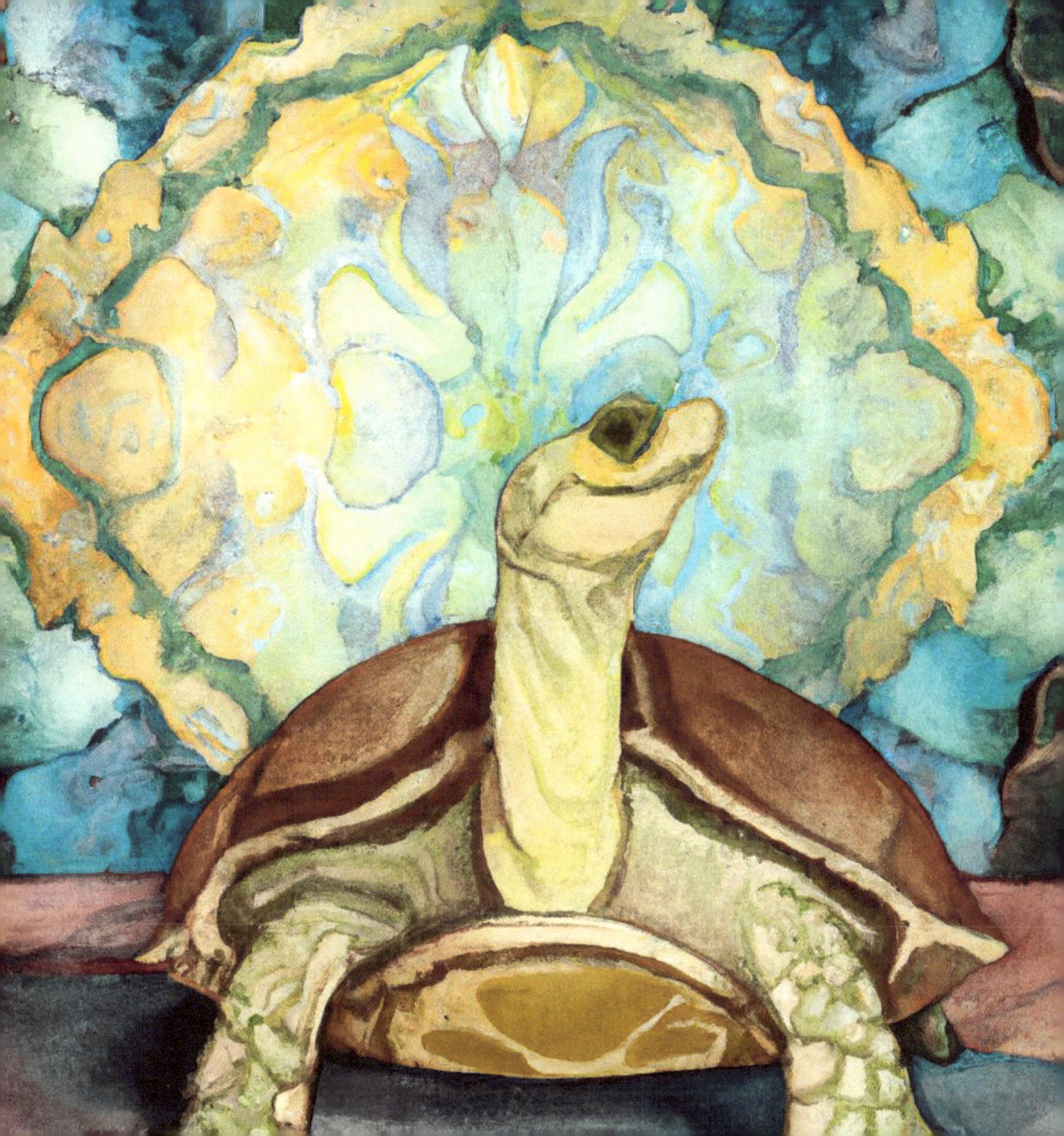

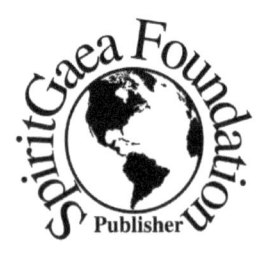

**Original Art
by Jeri Lee**

Copyright Jerilee.com
2022
All rights Reserved

Author Artist

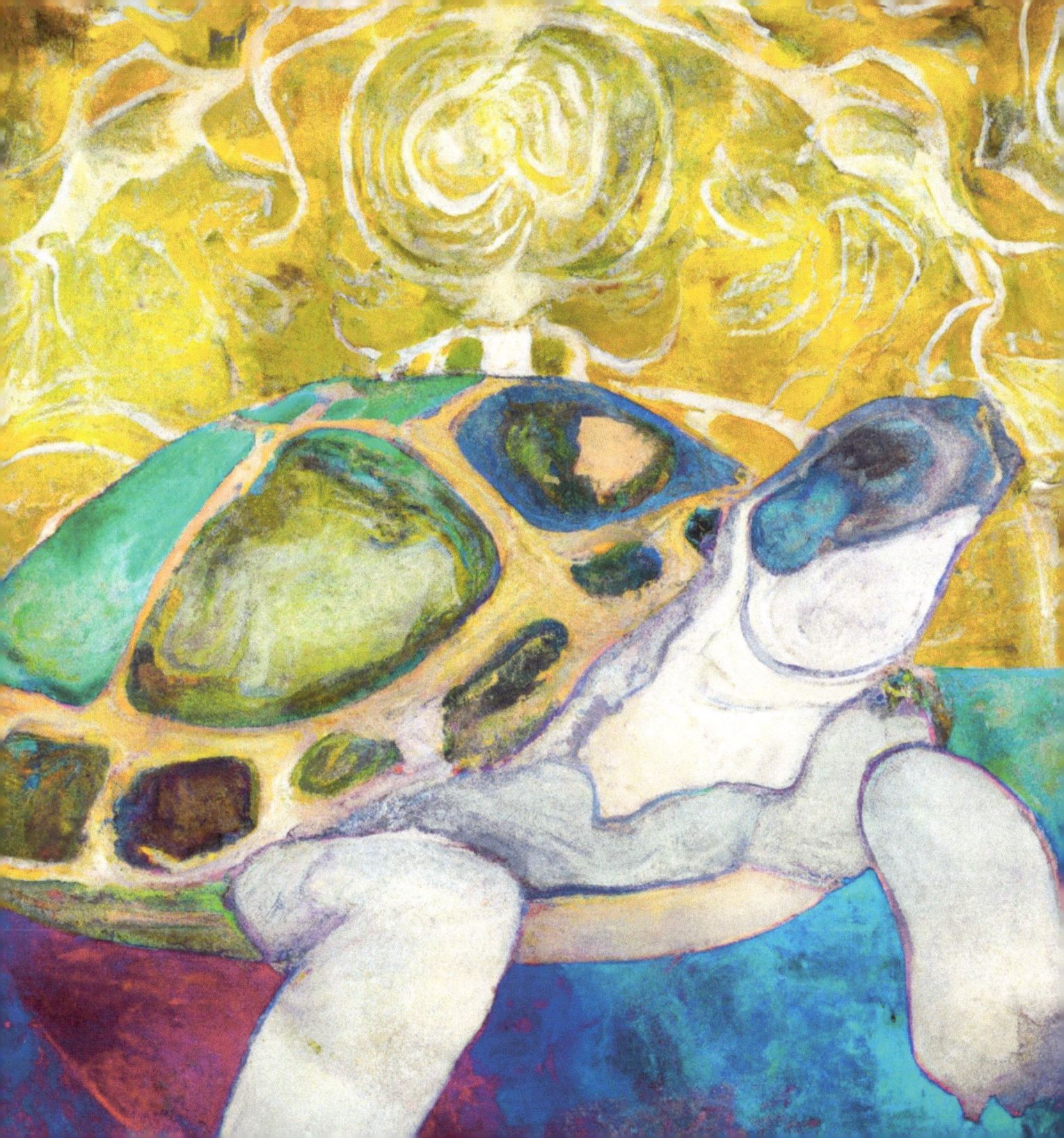

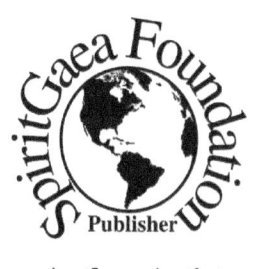

Author Artist

**Original Art
by Jeri Lee**

Copyright Jerilee.com
2022
All rights Reserved

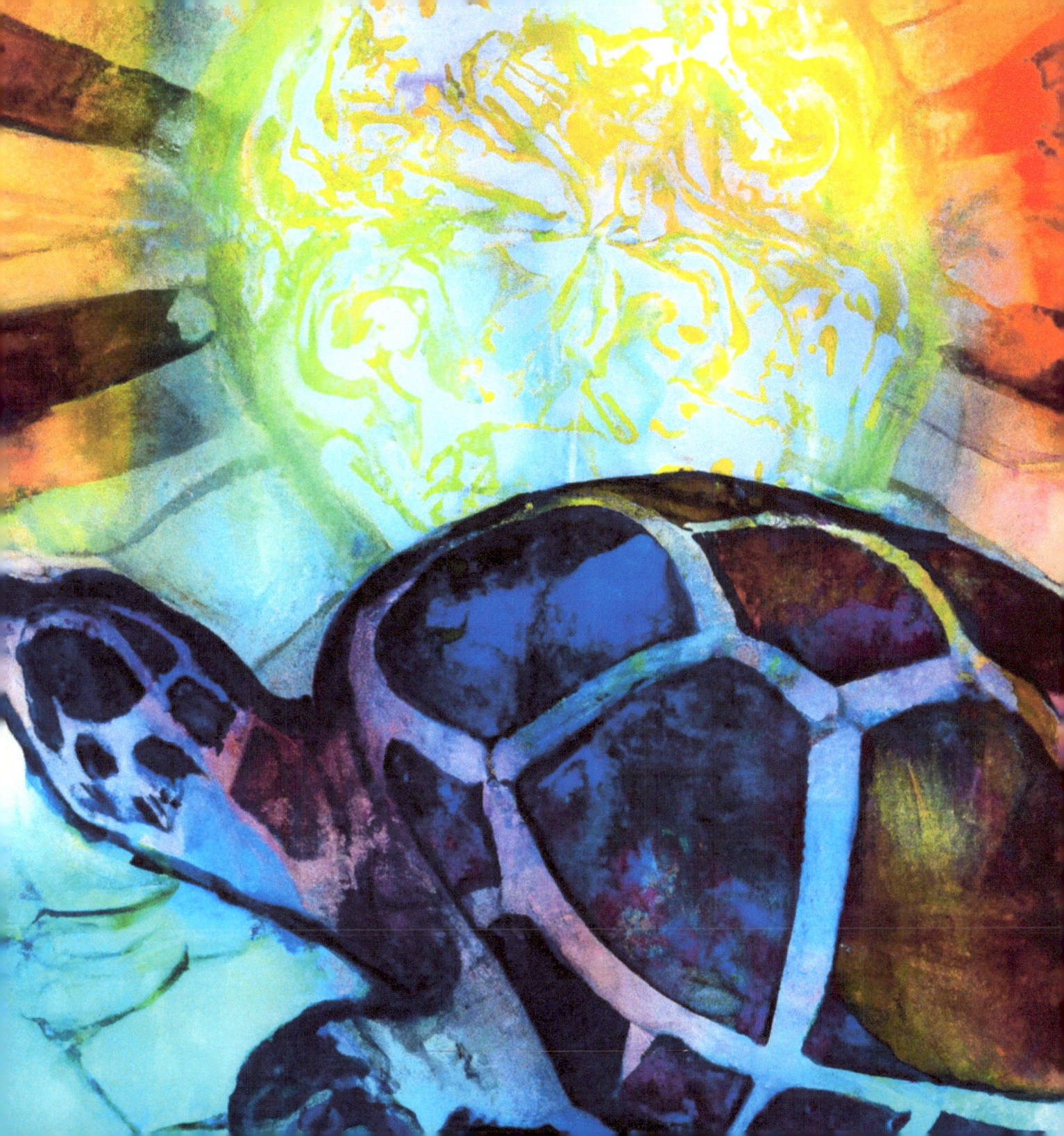

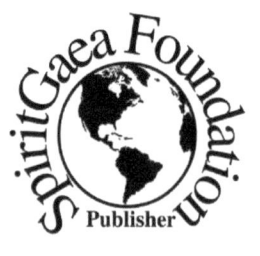

Author Artist

**Original Art
by Jeri Lee**

Copyright Jerilee.com
2022
All rights Reserved

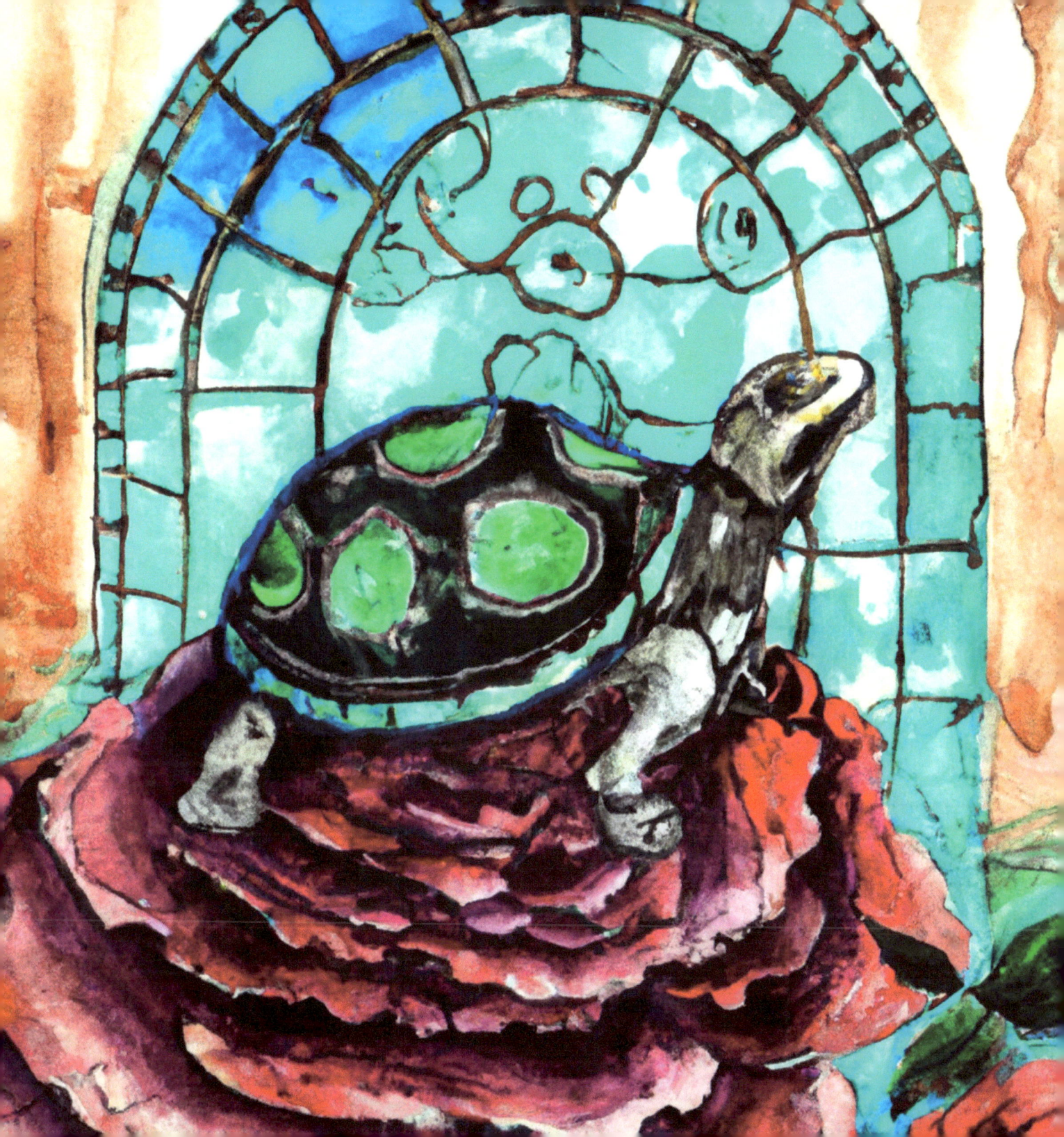

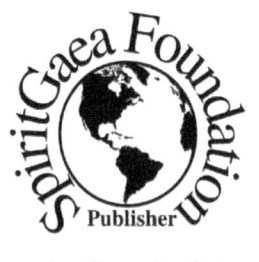

Original Art
by Jeri Lee

Copyright Jerilee.com
2022
All rights Reserved

Author Artist

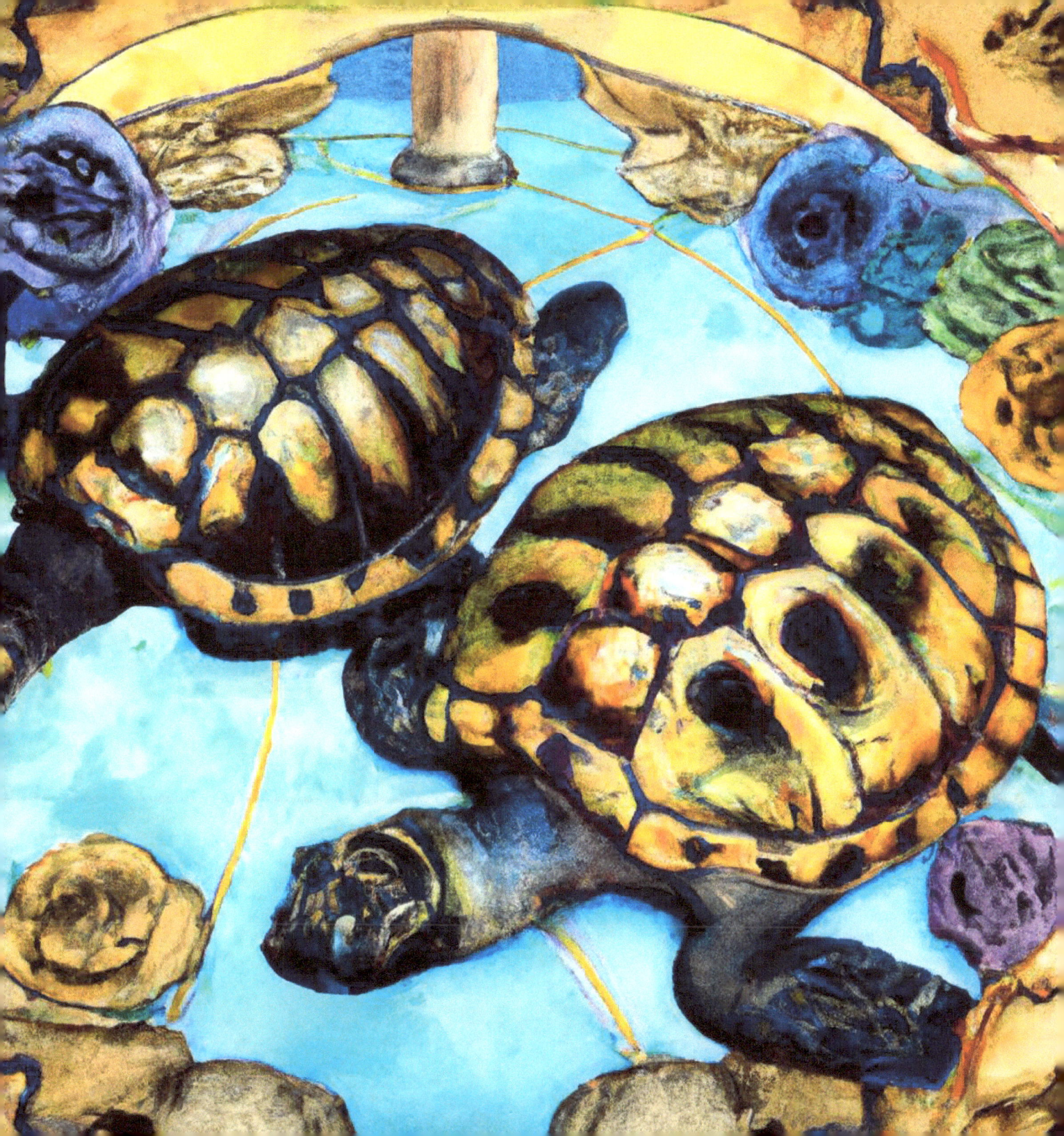

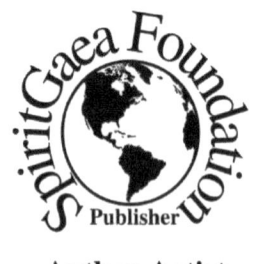

Author Artist

**Original Art
by Jeri Lee**

Copyright Jerilee.com
2022
All rights Reserved

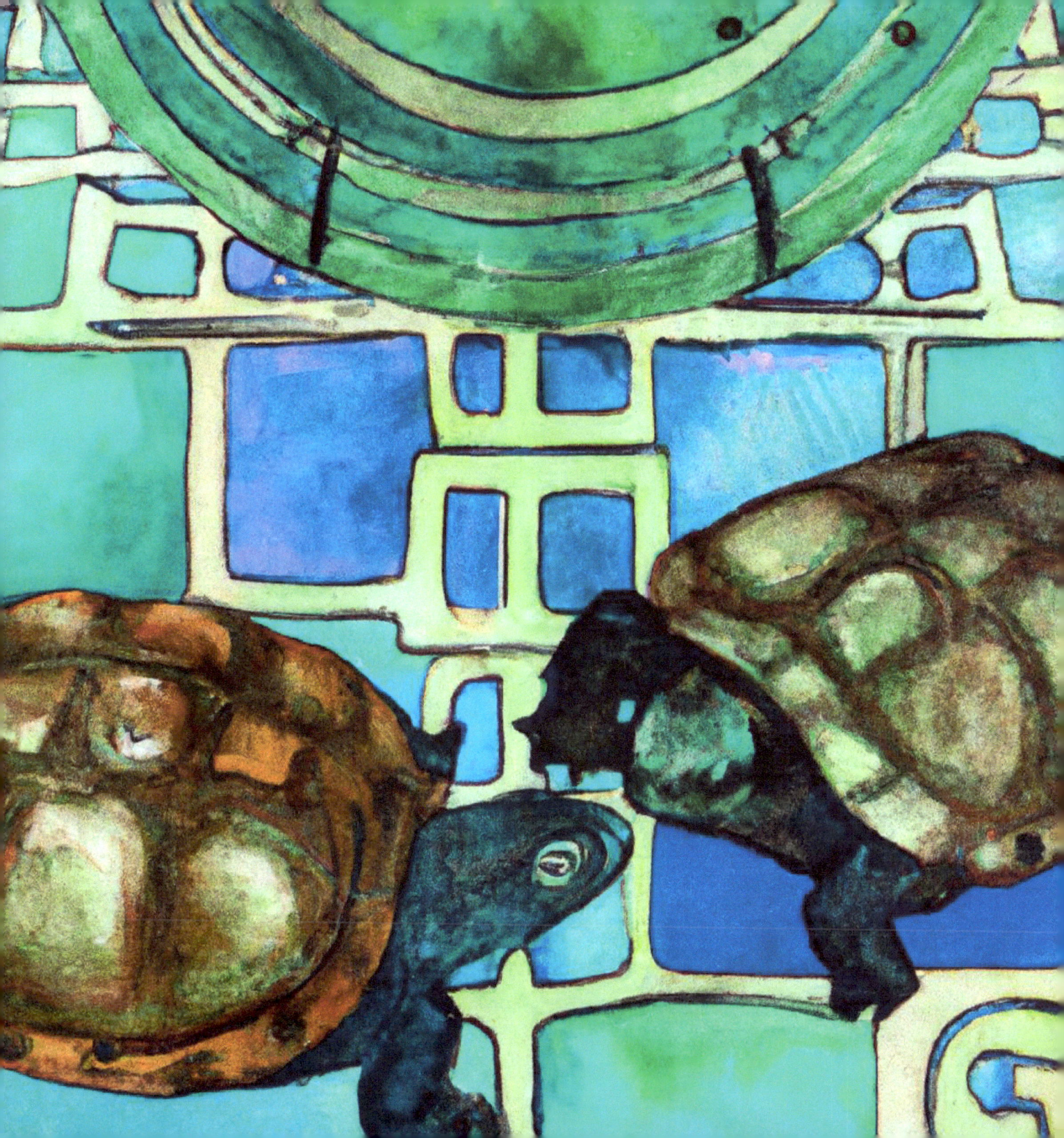

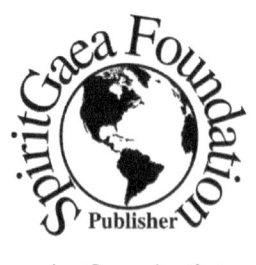

**Original Art
by Jeri Lee**

Copyright Jerilee.com
2022
All rights Reserved

Author Artist

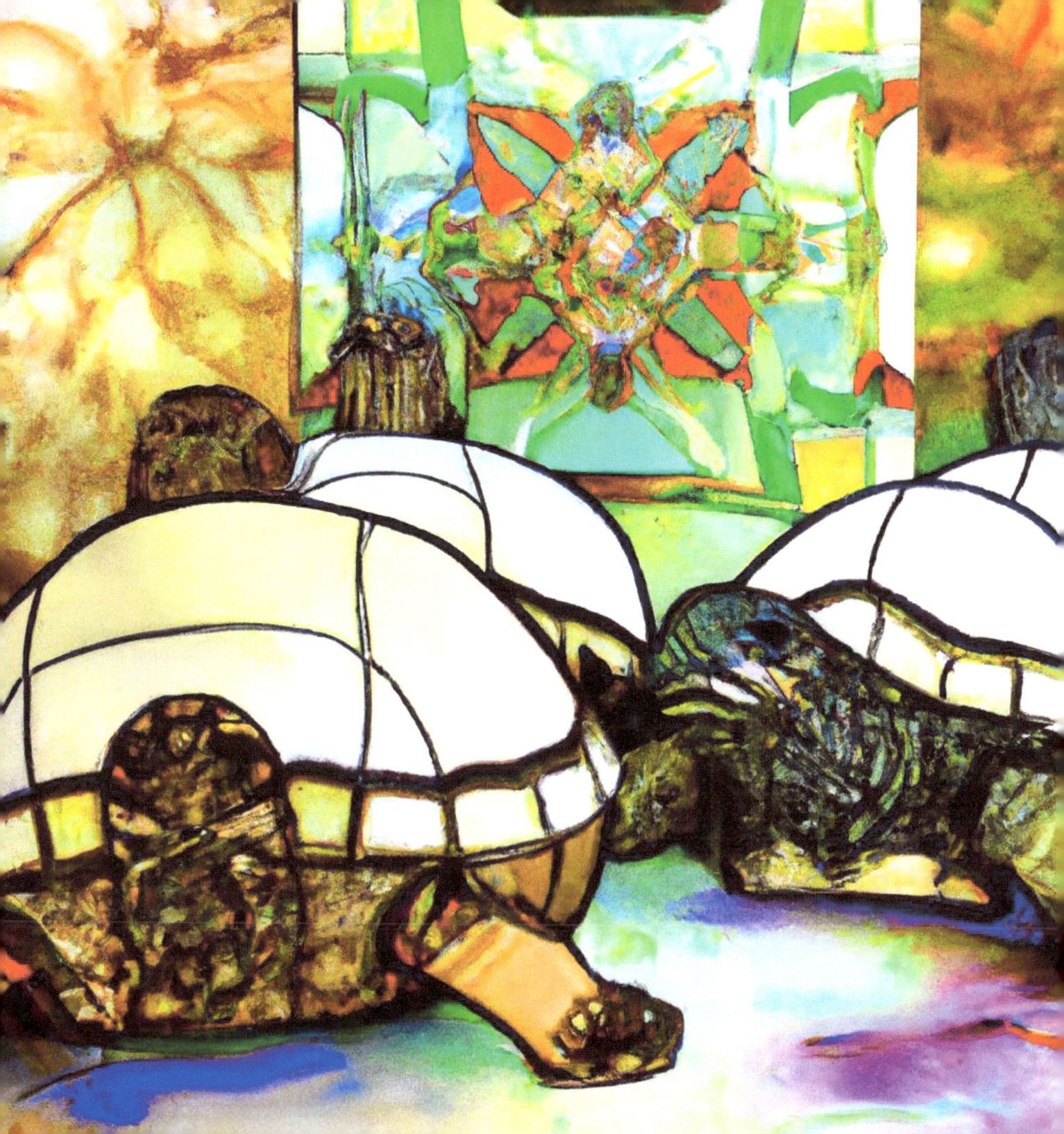

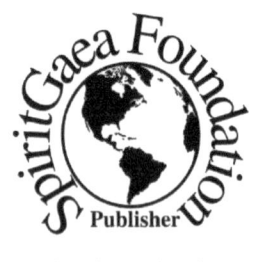

Author Artist

**Original Art
by Jeri Lee**

Copyright Jerilee.com
2022
All rights Reserved

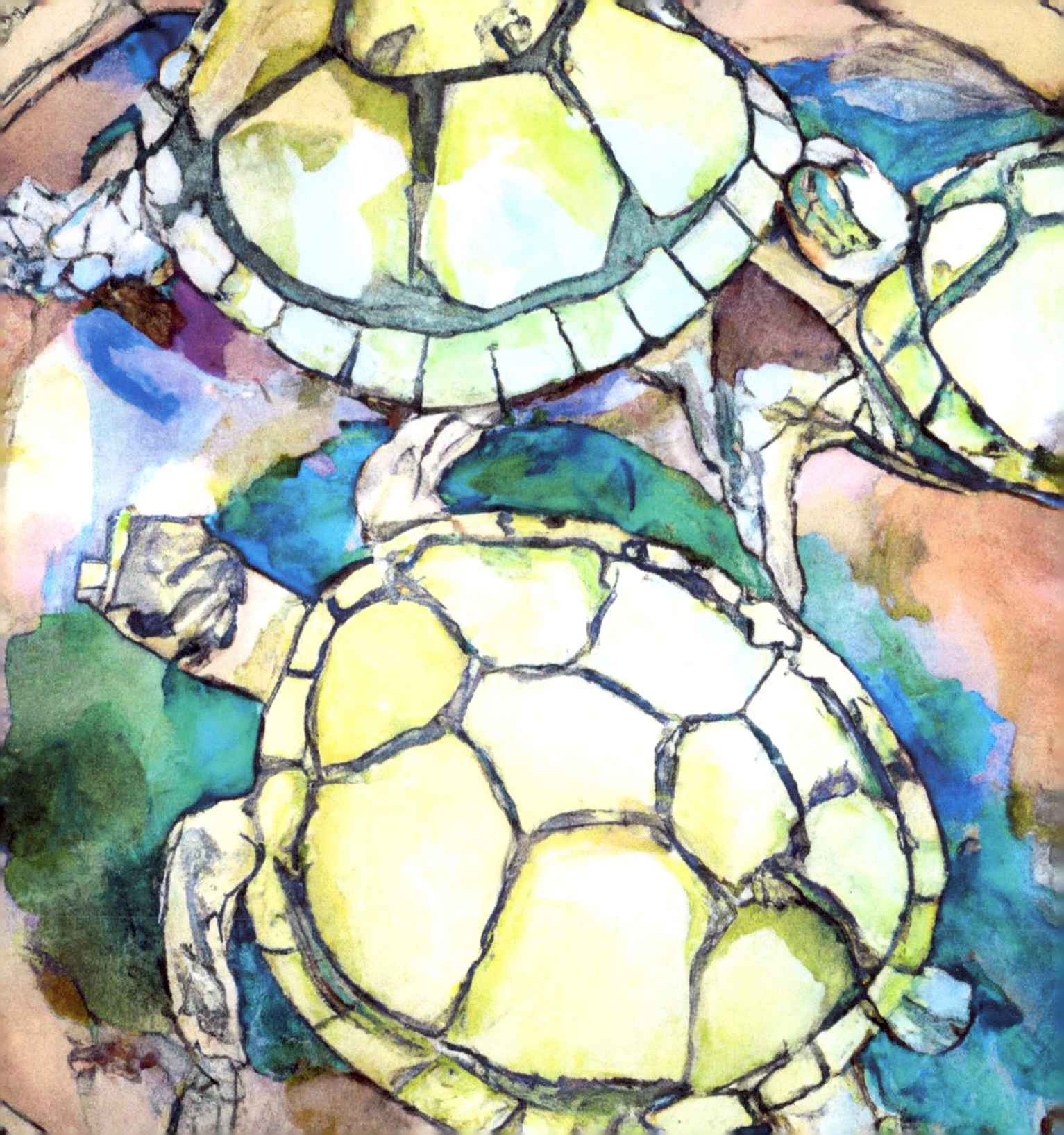

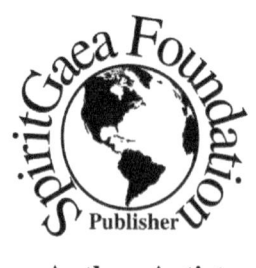

**Original Art
by Jeri Lee**

Copyright Jerilee.com
2022
All rights Reserved

Author Artist

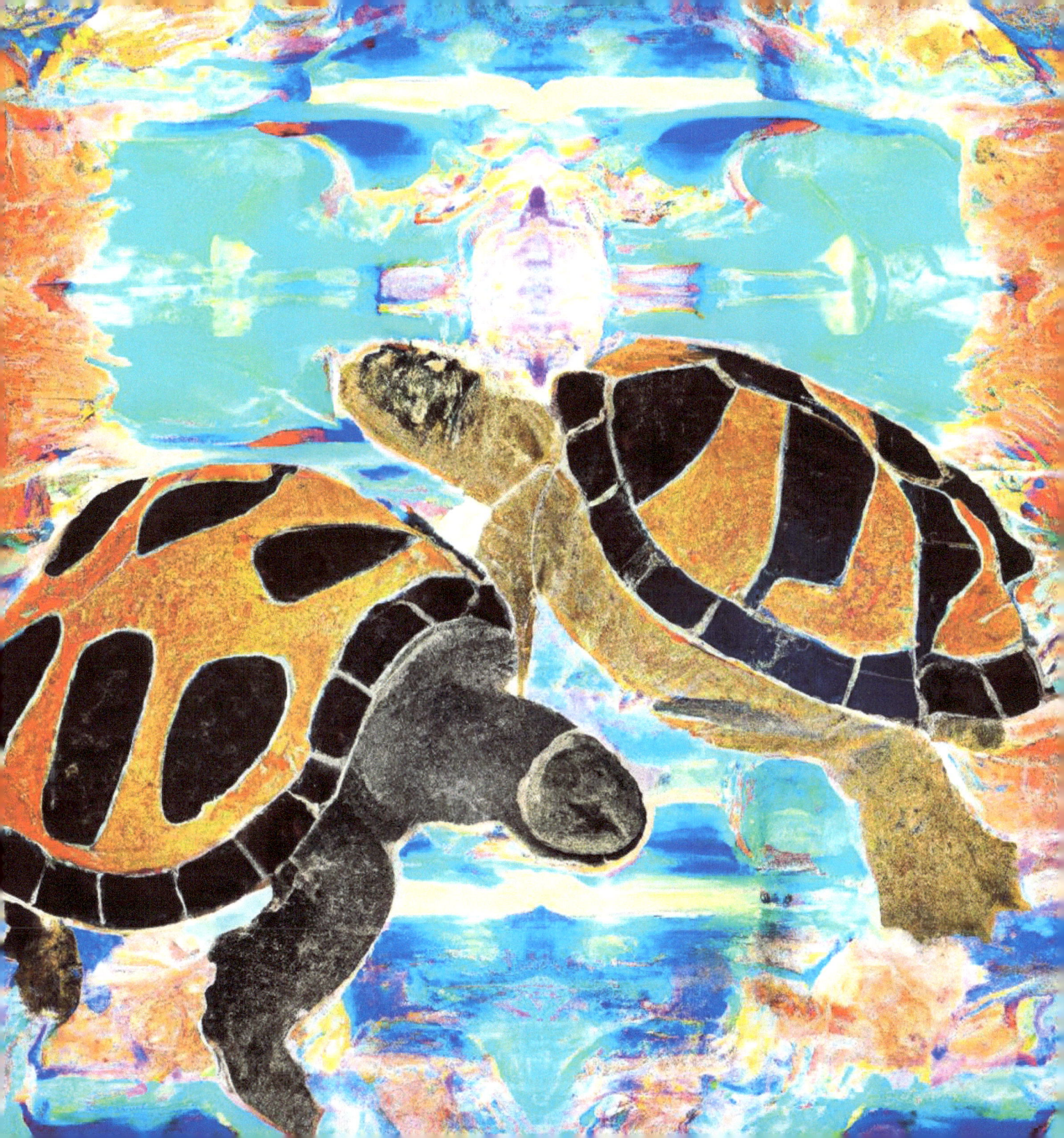

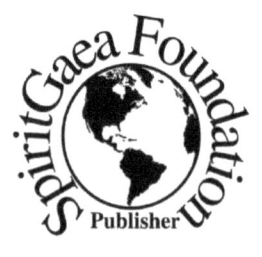

Author Artist

**Original Art
by Jeri Lee**

Copyright Jerilee.com
2022
All rights Reserved

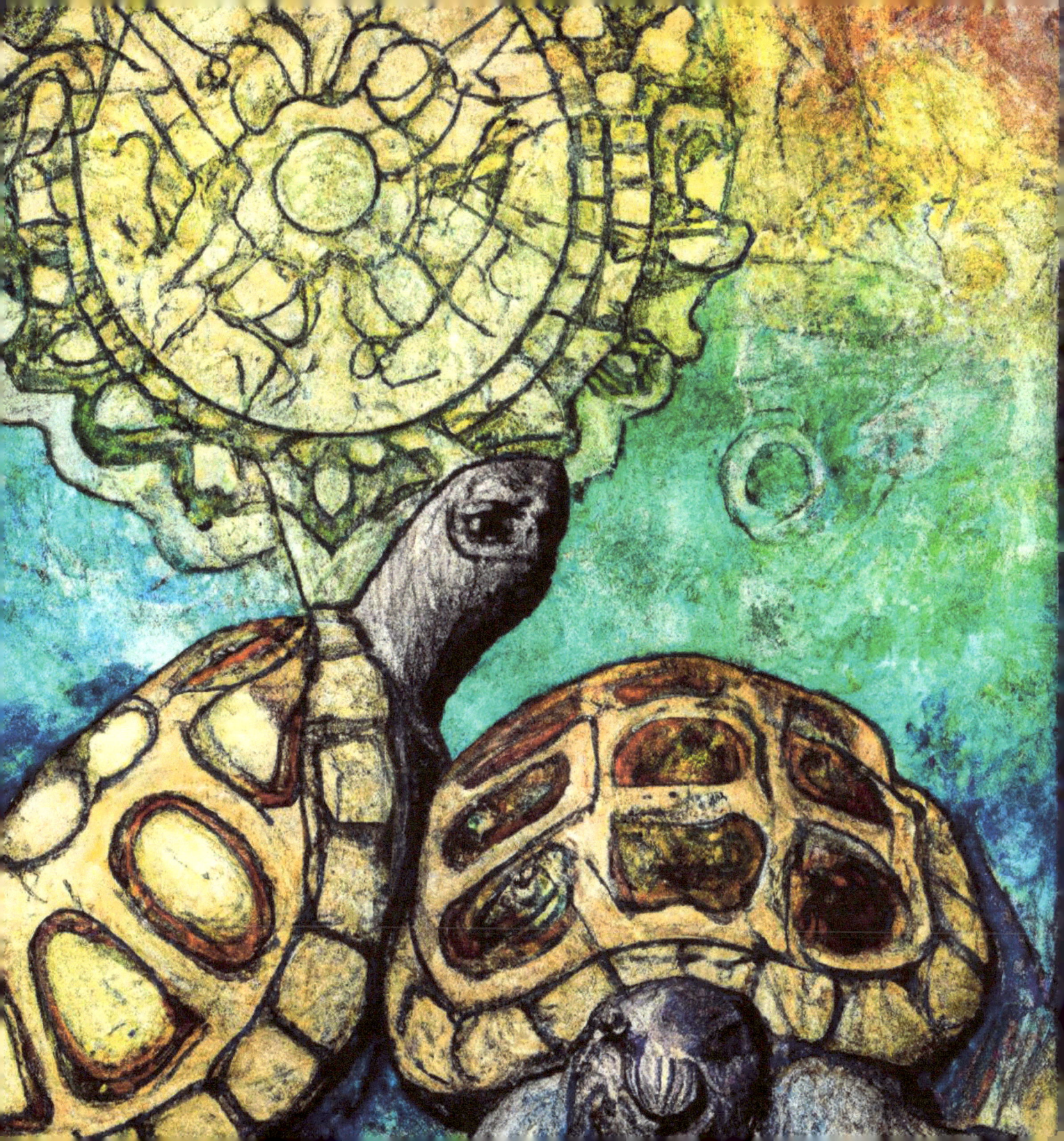

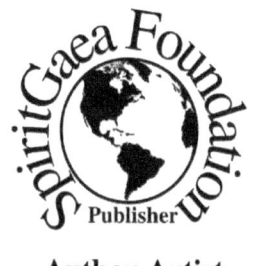

Author Artist

**Original Art
by Jeri Lee**

Copyright Jerilee.com
2022
All rights Reserved

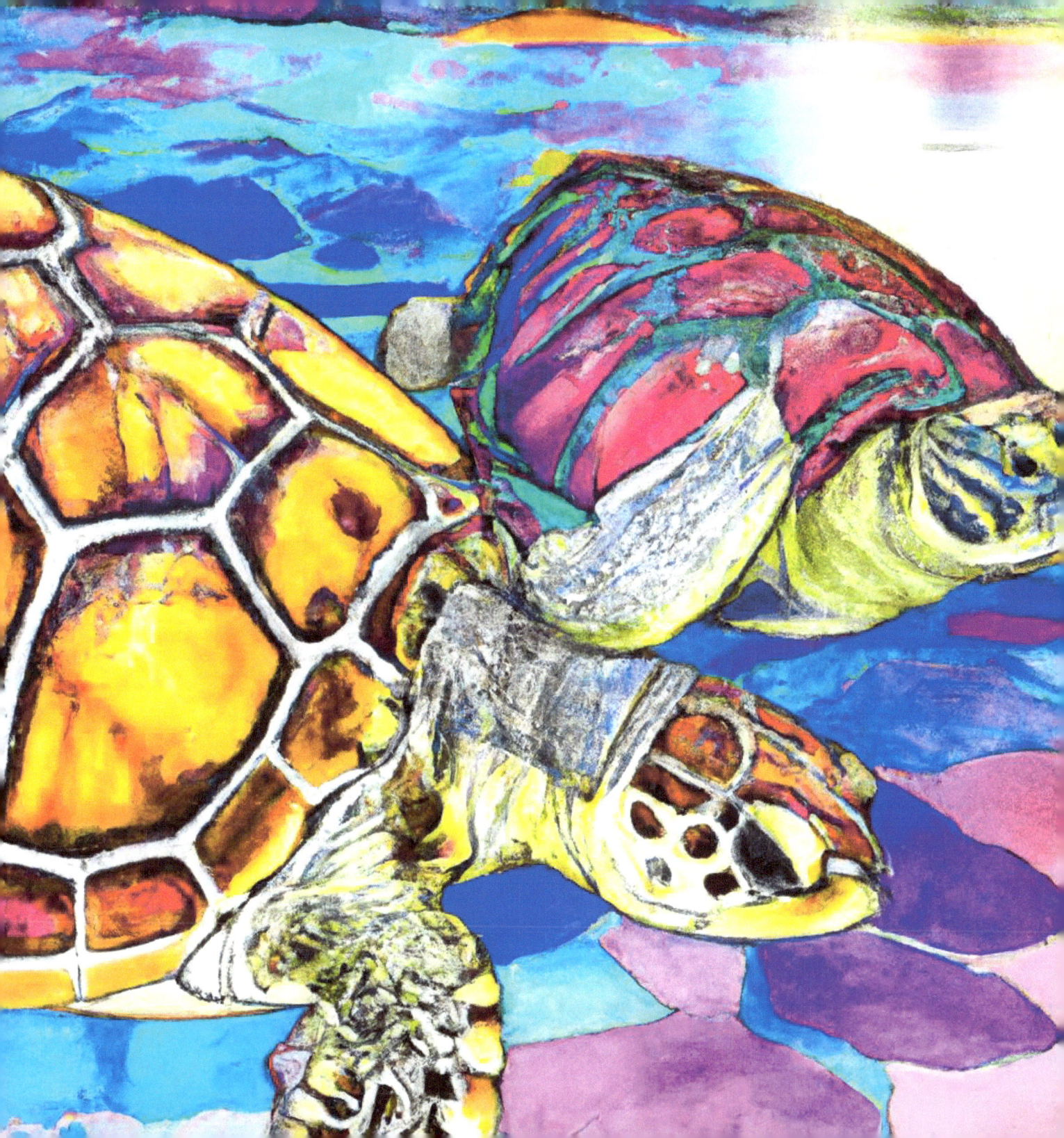

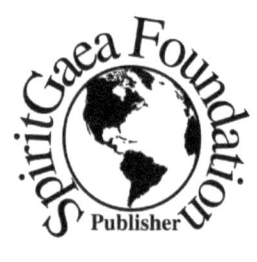

**Original Art
by Jeri Lee**

Copyright Jerilee.com
2022
All rights Reserved

Author Artist

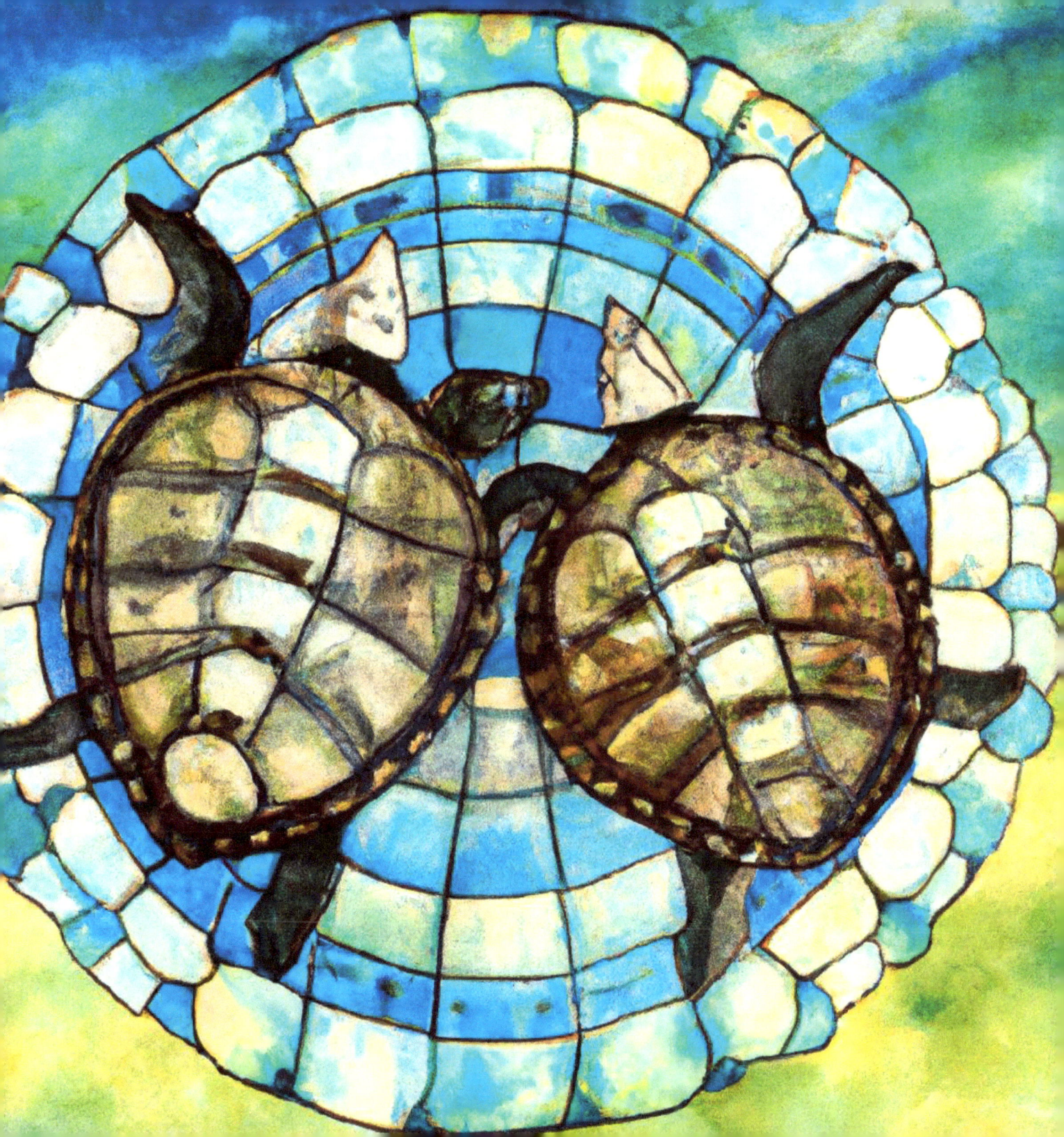

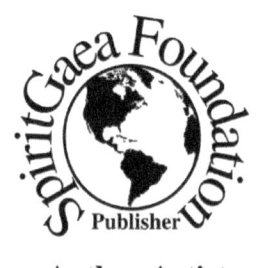

Author Artist

**Original Art
by Jeri Lee**

Copyright Jerilee.com
2022
All rights Reserved

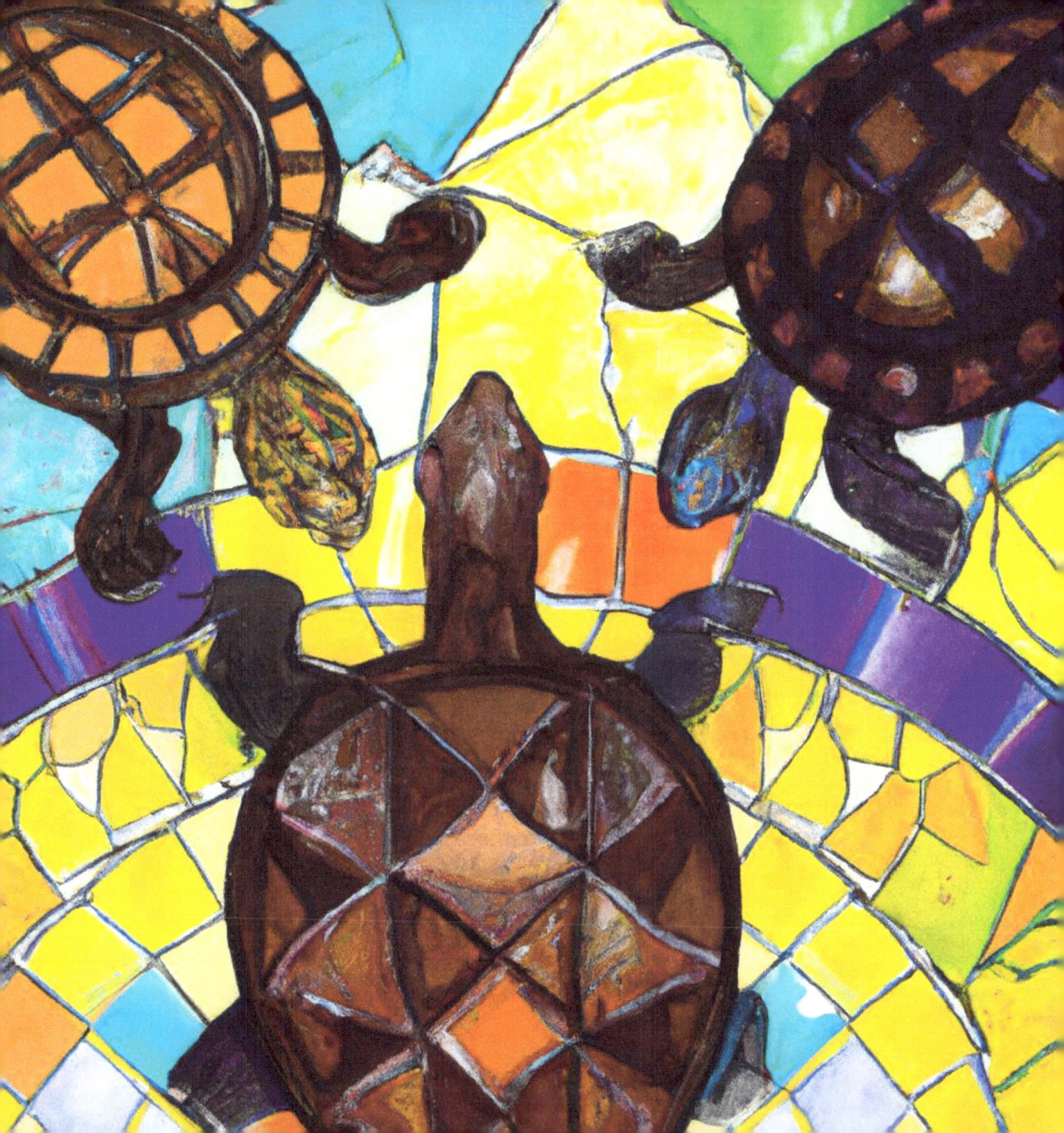

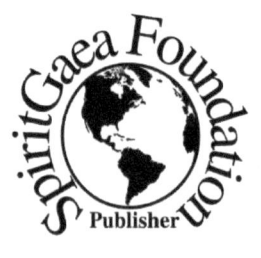

**Original Art
by Jeri Lee**

Copyright Jerilee.com
2022
All rights Reserved

Author Artist

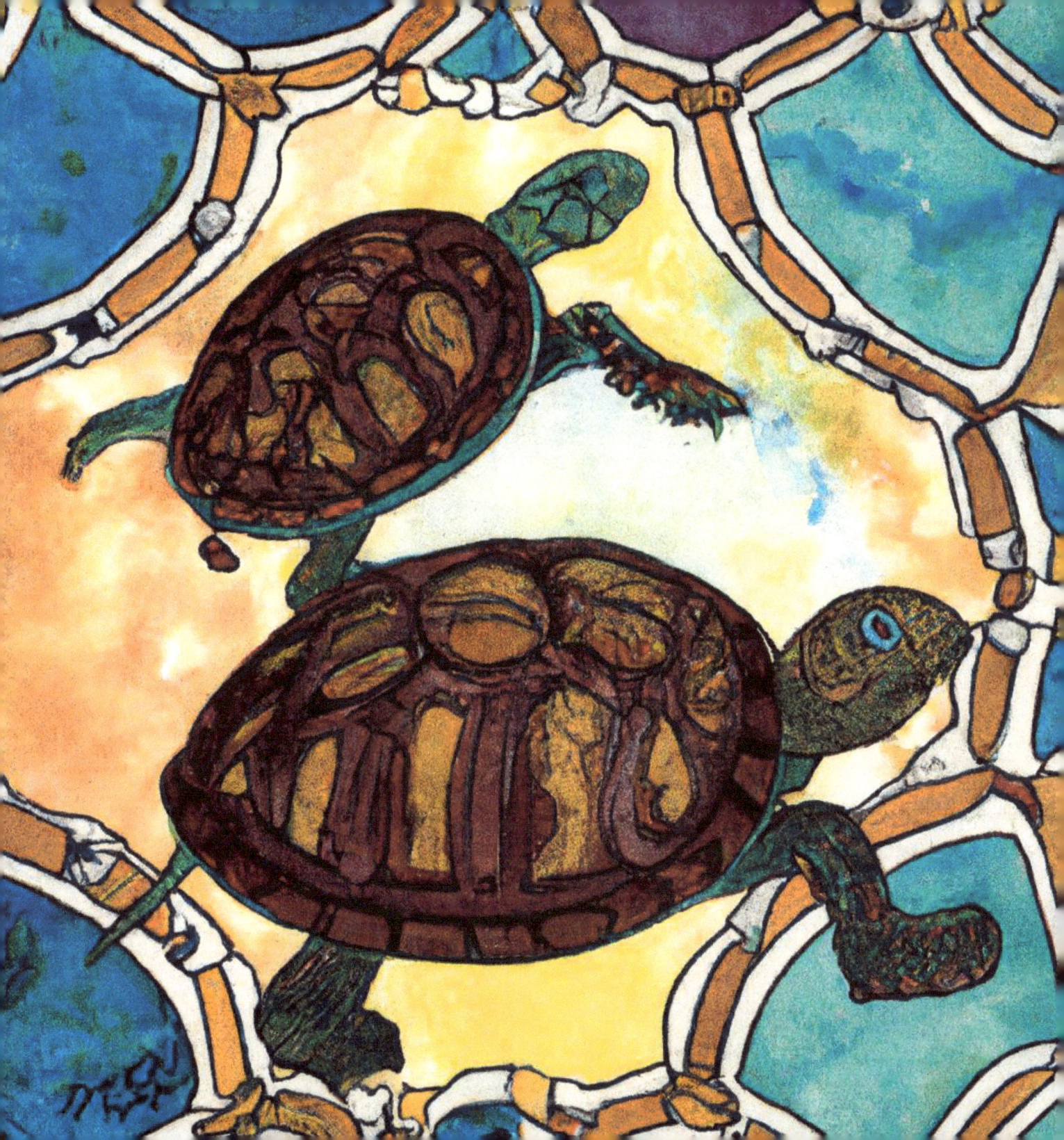

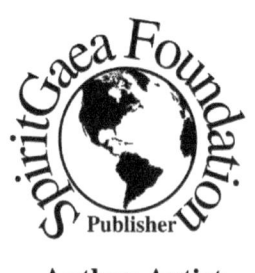

Author Artist

**Original Art
by Jeri Lee**

Copyright Jerilee.com
2022
All rights Reserved

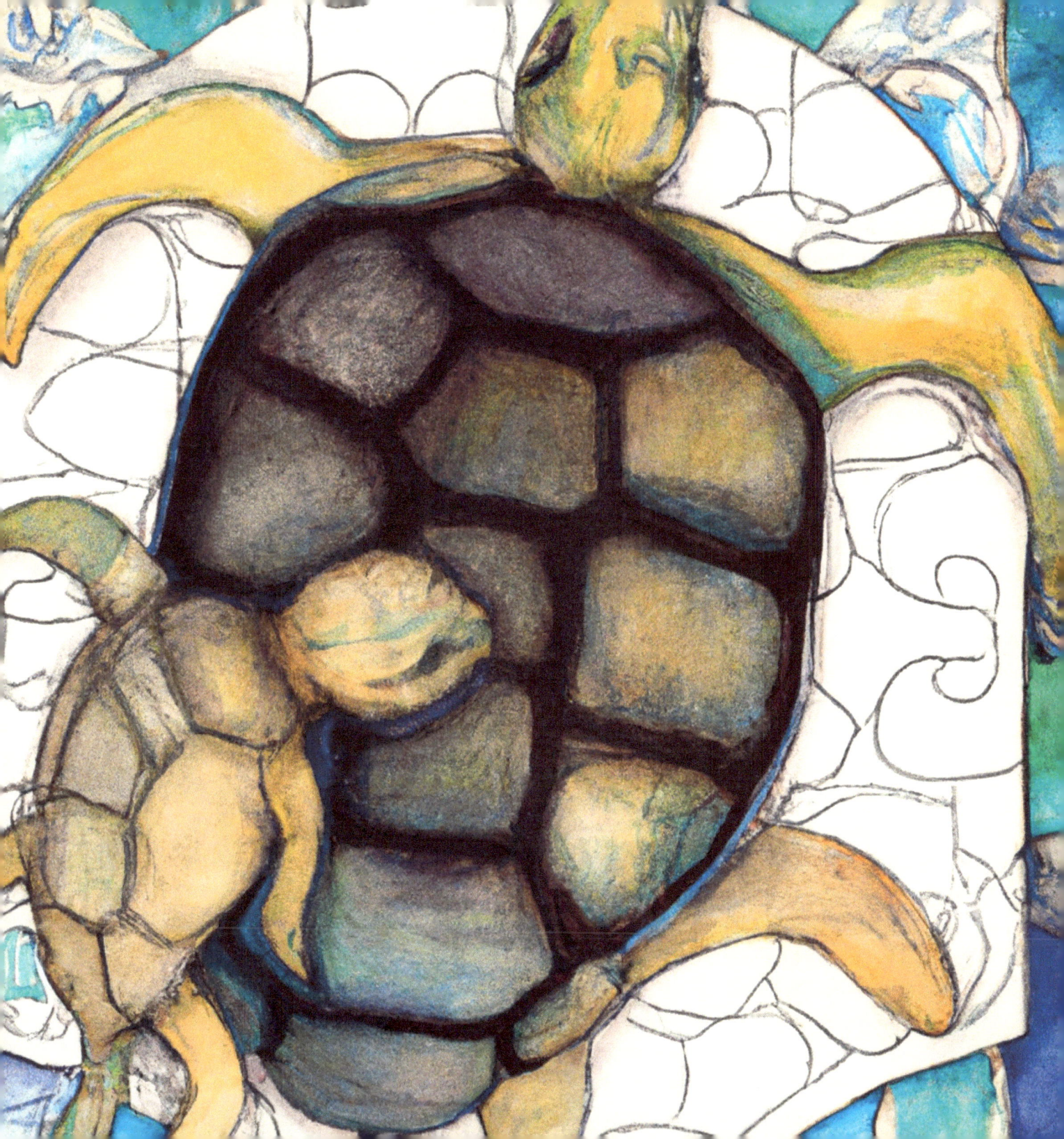

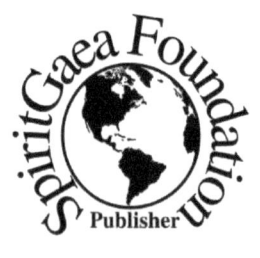

Author Artist

**Original Art
by Jeri Lee**

Copyright Jerilee.com
2022
All rights Reserved

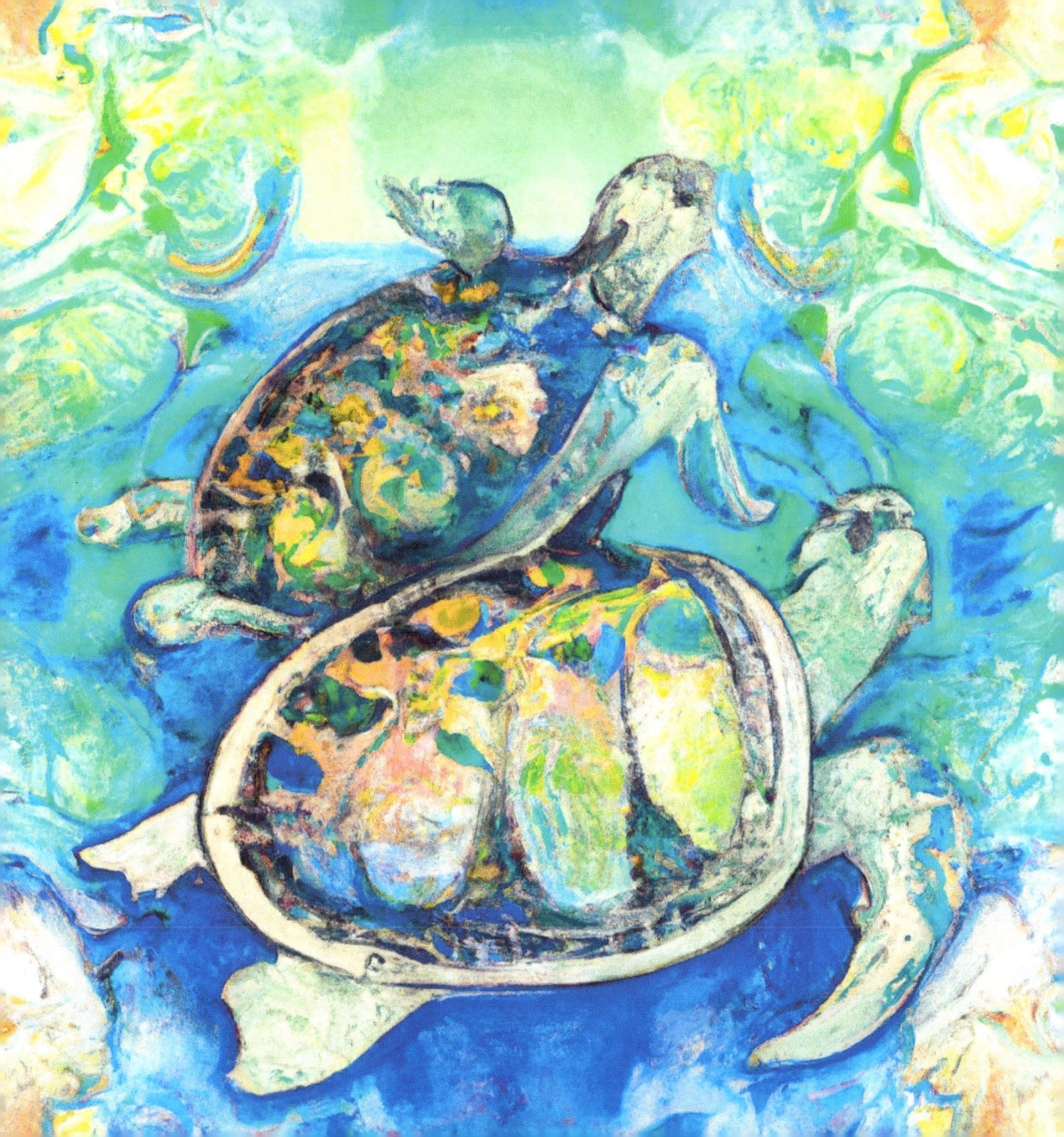

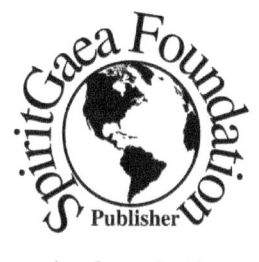

Author Artist

**Original Art
by Jeri Lee**

Copyright Jerilee.com
2022
All rights Reserved

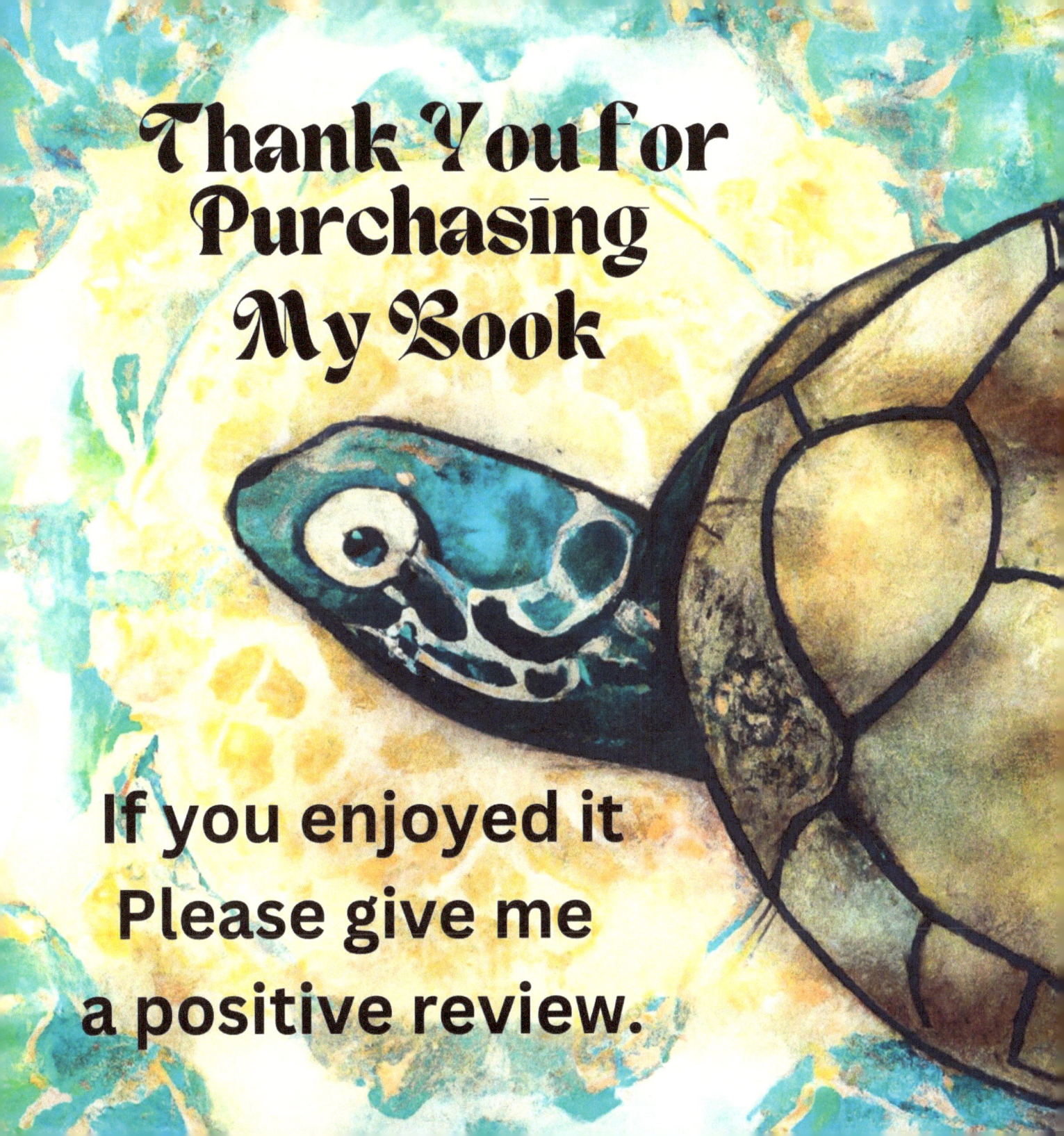

You Might enjoy one of my many coloring books, Most of which are designed with Adults in mind.

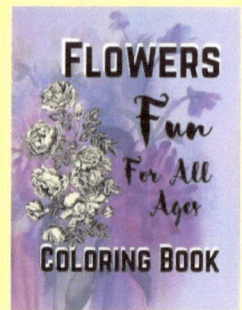
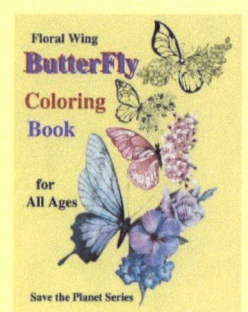
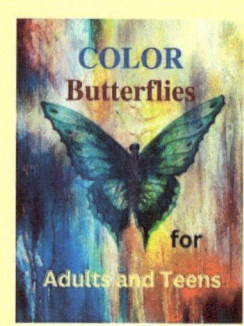
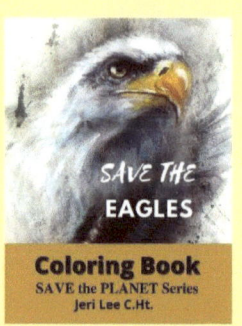
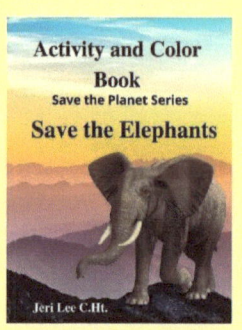
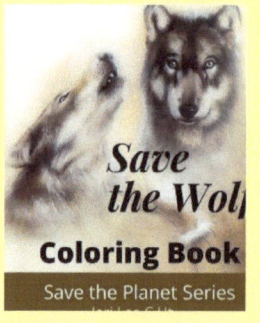
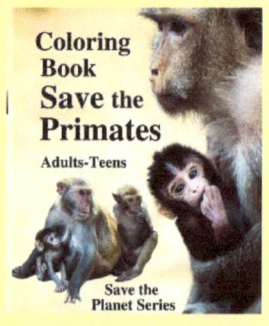
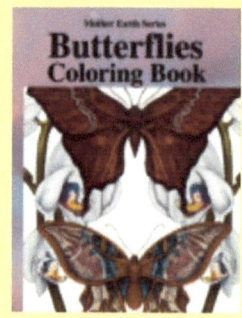
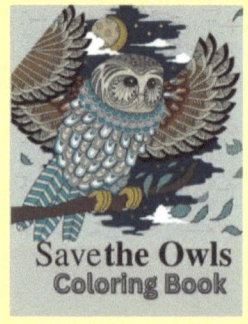
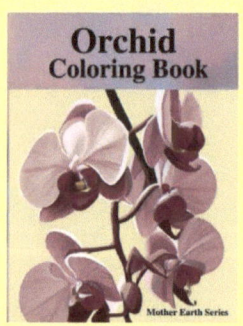
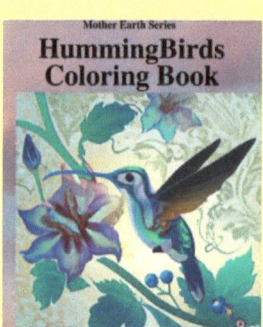
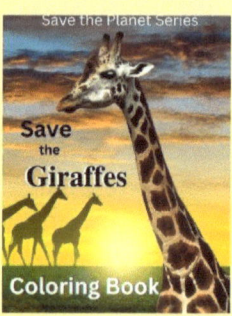
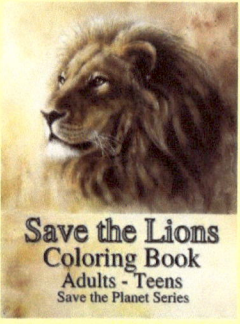

My Coloring books are 8.5 x 11 with 50 to 100 pages to color. They are focused on Save the Planet and pages can be view on my website. www,jerilee.com   purchases on Amazon.com

SINGING IN THE BRAIN

How to use Meditation, Visualization and Self-Hypnosis to Sing Yourself Healthy

JERI LEE C.HT.

About the Artist-Author

I was born in 1939 with an overactive ambition that even death could not alter. I have died twice but refuse to stay dead. I wrote Singiiing in the brain as a self-help book to share what I do to stay alive even in my 80s. From early life, pushing a pen or a brush has been my way of life.

Singing in the Brain

By using Meditation, Visualization and Self-Hypnosis you can sing yourself healthy. You utilize your right brain functions when you sing. Your voice is your best friend and is your natural tranquilizer so stay happy and healthy by singing to yourself. This is the true story of Author Jeri Lee, showing how she developed this process. This is a do it yourself book on finding your fountain of youth

t

Please Check out some of my other Prints

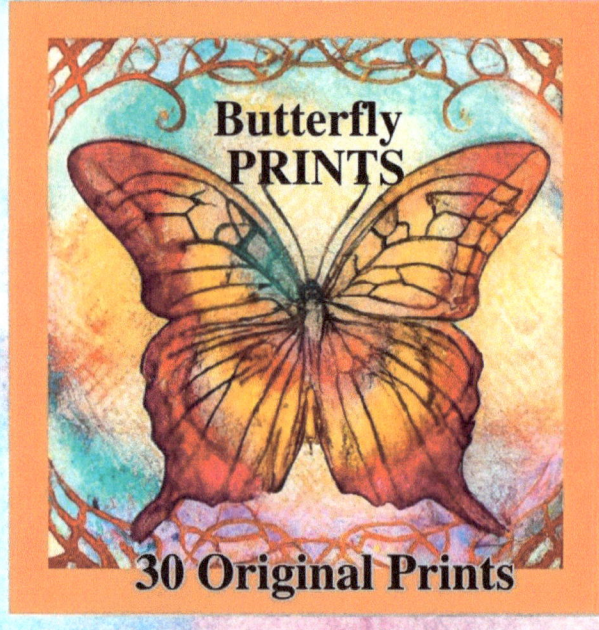

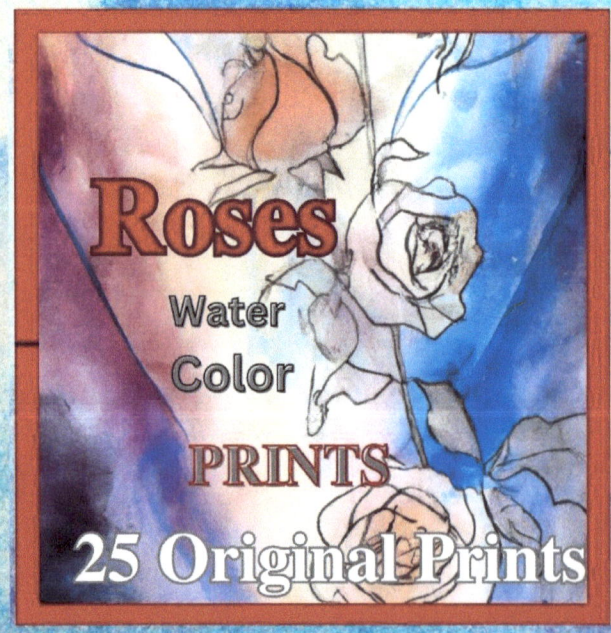

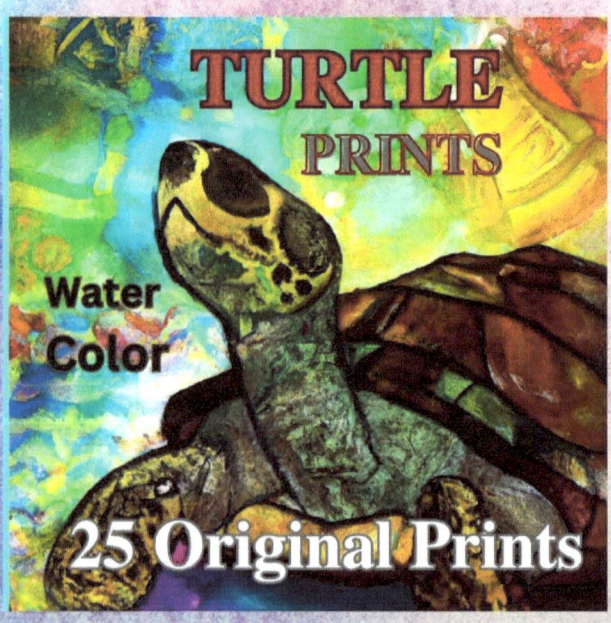

www.ingramcontent.com/pod-product-compliance
Lightning Source LLC
Chambersburg PA
CBHW041933240526
45473CB00034B/997